Project Management Inst.

Impact on Project Management of Allied Disciplines:

Trends and Future of Project Management Practices and Research

Thank you for your
valuable contributions.

Youngn Kwa
Frank Anbari

Project Management Institute

IMPACT ON PROJECT MANAGEMENT OF ALLIED DISCIPLINES:

TRENDS AND FUTURE OF PROJECT MANAGEMENT PRACTICES AND RESEARCH

Young Hoon Kwak, PhD
Frank T. Anbari, PhD, PMP

ISBN: 978-1-933890-45-6

Published by: Project Management Institute, Inc.
                        14 Campus Blvd
                        Newtown Square, PA 19073-3299 USA.
                        Phone: +610-356-4600
                        Fax: +610-356-4647
                        E-mail: customercare@pmi.org
                        Internet: www.pmi.org

PMI Publications welcomes corrections and comments on its books. Please feel free to send comments on typographical, formatting, or other errors. Simply make a copy of the relevant page of the book, mark the error, and send it to: Book Editor, PMI Publications, 14 Campus Blvd, Newtown Square, PA 19073-3299 USA.

To inquire about discounts for resale or educational purposes, please contact the PMI Book Service Center.

                        PMI Book Service Center
                        P.O. Box 932683, Atlanta, GA 31193-2683 USA
                        Phone: 1-866-276-4764 (within the U.S. or Canada)
                            or +1-770-280-4129 (globally)
                        Fax: +1-770-280-4113
                        E-mail: book.orders@pmi.org

10   9   8   7   6   5   4   3   2   1

Acknowledgements

This research work was partially funded by a research grant from the Project Management Institute, whose support is greatly appreciated.

We would like to thank all participants in the survey and the face-to-face and telephone interviews conducted during this research project. In particular, we wish to thank our esteemed colleagues Ernest Forman, Mary Granger, Alan Harpham, Ed Hoffman, Srinivas Prasad, Karl Pringle, Rodney Turner, and Stuart Umpleby for sharing their time, thoughts, and visions.

We would like to thank The George Washington University (GWU) for its support of this research effort. In particular, we would like to thank GWU's Master of Science in Project Management students, Mr. Ifechukwu Nduka, and Ms. Prarthana Sherchan for assisting in collecting and sorting data used in this study.

Finally, we would like to thank the staff of the research and publications departments of the Project Management Institute for their guidance and financial support during the processes of research and publication of this study. Any opinions, findings, conclusions, or recommendations expressed in this research are those of the authors and do not necessarily reflect the views of the Project Management Institute.

Table of Contents

LIST OF FIGURES

LIST OF TABLES

Executive Summary

Project management has been practiced for thousands of years, but only recently have organizations begun to apply systematic and scientific tools and techniques to manage complex projects. Today's approaches to project management can be traced to methodologies designed by the U.S. Department of Defense in the years after World War II. Subsequent advances in management information systems have helped to codify project management practices. Most recently, the Internet has dramatically enhanced the ability of individuals, teams and organizations to manage projects across continents and cultures in real time.

Project management has been greatly influenced by allied disciplines and in return it influenced them. Therefore, innovative theories, trends and challenges being learned from investigating project management allied disciplines could have important implications and applications in the future of project management. Researchers and practitioners adapted different academic disciplines to contribute to the body of knowledge in project management. Network scheduling techniques, decision-making tools and resource allocation and optimization approaches came from the management science discipline. Organizational dynamics theories provided insights and recognized the benefits of project-driven organizations. Organizational behavior and development issues, such as motivation, leadership, and conflict resolution, influenced and are being influenced by project management.

We identified eight allied disciplines of project management:

- Operations Research, Decision Sciences, Operation Management and Supply Chain Management (OR/DS/OM/SCM),
- Organizational Behavior and Human Resources Management (OB/HRM),
- Information Technology and Information Systems (IT/IS),
- Technology, Innovation, New Product Development and Research and Development (TECH/INNOV/NPD/R&D),
- Engineering-Construction, Contracts, Legal Aspects and Expert Witness (EC/CONTRACT/LEGAL),

- Strategy, Integration, Portfolio Management, Value of Project Management and Marketing (STRATEGY/PPM),
- Performance Management, Earned Value Management, Project Finance and Accounting (PERFORMANCE/EVM), and
- Quality Management, Six Sigma, and Process Improvement (QM/6SIGMA/PI).

We selected 18 top management and business journals for in-depth analysis:

Academy of Management
- *AOM Perspectives/Executives*
- *AOM Journal*
- *AOM Review*

INFORMS
- *Operations Research*
- *Management Science*
- *Organization Science*
- *Information Systems Research*
- *Interfaces*

Practitioner
- *Harvard Business Review*
- *California Management Review*
- *Sloan Management Review*
- *Long Range Planning*

IEEE Engineering Management Society
- *IEEE Transactions on Engineering Management*

Other Journals
- *Journal of Operations Management*
- *MIS Quarterly*
- *Strategic Management Journal*
- *Administrative Science Quarterly*
- *Journal of Small Business*

We analyzed past, current and future trends of project management research trends as follows:

- We selected 18 top management and business journals and analyzed articles published between the 1950s and June 2007 that addressed project management in the eight allied disciplines. Based on the 537 papers that we investigated, we coded each paper in up to three disciplines (categories). In some cases, papers were coded for only one or two combined categories. Based on this coding scheme, we identified and analyzed 980 total occurrences in the 537 papers using the eight allied disciplines. We also designed and administered a survey of the project management community and collected data about the availability of knowledge and information regarding the allied disciplines and their impact on project management by decade, as well as thoughts and opinions on the impact, trends, and future of project management. Finally, we conducted face-to-face and telephone, in-depth interviews with selected allied disciplines and project management researchers, scholars, and practitioners and further identified the trends, challenges, and future of the project management discipline and the impact of allied disciplines on it.

We found the following results:

Analysis of 18 Management and Business Journals

- Overall, there is a strong, positive publications trend of project management related research in all selected 18 journals. Regression analysis shows a strong, positive upward trend in project management research publications in the allied disciplines. Publications related to project management research in the allied disciplines in the selected 18 journals started to increase substantially beginning in the 1980s. In fact, over 80% of the papers were published after 1980. By the 1990s, project management related papers had appeared in every journal on the list.
- The top four journals (*IEEE Transactions on Engineering Management, Management Science, Long Range Planning, and Harvard Business Review*) published more than 50% of the total papers related to project management.

Analysis of Allied Disciplines

- We have seen an explosion of popularity and strong interest in project management research starting from the 1980s, and the trends are likely to continue in the future. There are more occurrences of project management in the allied disciplines in papers published in the selected 18 journals starting from the 1980s (19%), 1990s (30%) and continuing in the 2000s (31%) showing a greater interest in project management research in the allied disciplines.
- Ranking of occurrences of the eight disciplines from most to the least appeared subjects over the last 50 years is:
  1. STRATEGY/PPM (30%)
  2. OR/DS/OM/SCM (23%)
  3. OB/HRM (13%)
  4. IT/IS (11%)
  5. TECH/INNOV/NPD/R&D (11%)

6. PERFORMANCE/EVM (7%)
7. EC/CONTRACT/LEGAL (3%)
8. QM/6SIGMA/PI (2%)

- STRATEGY/PPM, TECH/INNOV/NPD/R&D, IT/IS, and PERFORMANCE/EVM are the four disciplines that show large increases in occurrences in publications and are expected to continue to have strong upward trends in publication of project management related research in the foreseeable future. These four areas represent the disciplines in which scholars' research interests are currently focused and appear to have great research potential in the future.
- Occurrences in publication of project management related research in the areas of OR/DS/OM/SCM and OB/HRM peaked during the 1990s and the occurrences have slowed down in the 2000s. These two disciplines are two of the origins of project management, and it seems that research output in these areas have matured with a possible continuing downward trend for OR/DS/OM/SCM in the future.
- EC/CONTRACT/LEGAL and QM/6SIGMA/PI did not really gain any momentum in occurrences of research output from the management research community. It is important to note that these two areas are having great success in publication in relevant journals in their fields, but appear to struggle when it comes to publication in the top management journals. Because of the practical nature of these two disciplines, it seems that the management scholars' community is strongly resisting acceptance of these two areas as mainstream management research.

Analysis of Survey
- Results of the survey showed generally that there is a growing trend in terms of both availability and impact of research and applications in the allied disciplines related to project management. These findings were validated through the face-to-face and telephone, in-depth interviews.
- Survey respondents indicated that OB/HRM, TECH/INNOV/NPD/R&D, STRATEGY/PPM, and OR/DS/OM/SCM were the four disciplines that respondents perceived as low on availability of related knowledge and low on impact related to project management. It could be interpreted that these four disciplines still have potential for more research (availability) and could have potential for greater influence (impact) in the future.
- PERFORMANCE/EVM and EC/CONTRACT/LEGAL were the two areas that respondents perceived as high in availability of related knowledge, but low on impact related to project

management. It could be interpreted that there is plenty of related information available currently; however, the impact on project management is low.

- QM/6SIGMA/PI and IT/IS were the two areas that were in the high availability and high impact quadrant. It could be interpreted that these two areas are the hot fields in project management currently.
- Survey respondents indicated that there was no discipline with low availability and high impact.

Gap Analysis between 18 Top Management and Business Journals and Project Management

- It is likely that research being published in top management and business journals may be setting the trends of impact on project management and its allied disciplines in the future.
- There are interesting differences between the perceptions of the project management community and the actual research publications trends of allied disciplines in the 18 top management and business journals. Rankings of occurrence/availability of the two sets of data contradict each other substantially. We do not believe that there is anything wrong with the results or data. Analysis of the results clearly shows that research interests and publications in top management and business journals and the availability of actual knowledge and information from the project management community's perspective are different. This is because the project management community relies on various sources of information besides top management journal articles.
- Research trends in the 18 top management and business journals vs. the current impact on project management as viewed by the project management community also had no direct relationship between them.
- There is visible divergence between the impact on project management of the eight allied disciplines from the perspective of the project management community and the number of occurrences in publications in the top management and business journals. In particular, none of the allied disciplines with high availability in the selected journals was indicated to have high impact on project management, which may highlight areas for relevant research and publications in areas of high current interest to the project management community. These observations may also highlight for management academic researchers and editors of the top management and business journals areas in which further knowledge needs to be developed and disseminated to support the dynamic and growing

discipline of project management and which will be viewed to have particular relevance in the project management community.

Future of Project Management's Allied Disciplines
- Despite the inherent limitations on analyzing and forecasting the future of the eight disciplines related to project management, analysis indicates that STRATEGY/PPM, OB/HRM, IT/IS, PERFORMANCE/EVM, and TECH/INNOV/NPD/R&D would have more availability in knowledge and information and have greater impact in the future. Analysis also showed that OR/DS/OM/SCM would have more availability in knowledge and information but the impact will remain the same in the future.
- The project management research trend of shifting from OR/DS/OM/SCM to OB/HRM has possibly reached its peak.
- IT/IS will continue to provide enhanced tools for project management, and will have a high impact in the future. As the IT/IS discipline matures, project management tools and techniques will continue to become available to general users, which makes it easier to implement project management principles.
- PERFORMANCE/EVM and related methods for measuring project performance will grow rapidly particularly due to governmental regulations requiring systematic cost/schedule evaluation in managing government projects.
- STRATEGY/PPM and QM/6SIGMA/PI should have a growing impact on project management, as business strategies are developed and qualities are measured and analyzed to plan and implement effective project management. For many organizations, the biggest gains that they see come from adapting and implementing STRATEGY/PPM and QM/6SIGMA/PI.
- TECH/INNOV/NPD/R&D and PERFORMANCE/EVM are poised to make major breakthroughs given the recent organizational interest and institutional determination on achieving project success.
- OR/DS/OM/SCM, PERFORMANCE/EVM, IT/IS, and TECH/INNOV/NPD/R&D will work together to deliver tools and techniques to allow the "science" of planning, scheduling, and cost control to function in a real project delivery environment.

Future Trends and Impacts of PM Practice and PM Research
- Project management has a lot to learn from allied disciplines. The project management community must understand that the allied disciplines are needed and must embrace and apply

them as part of project management. To do so, the project management community should be engaged in acquiring knowledge and participating in major activities of the allied disciplines to better understand the emerging and promising practices for future project endeavors. The practice of project management in different disciplines will increase the overall awareness of project management in many fields. The growing knowledge base will formalize the discipline of project management, increase the effectiveness, and influence new project management practices. Relevant knowledge developed in the allied disciplines will be integrated into project management. Requirements and advances of allied disciplines should drive development of new thoughts, processes, and procedures in project management.

- From the research standpoint, it is exciting to see how project management will be affected. From the integration of management fields new and interesting knowledge may emerge for the science, art, and practice of project management. Theoretical developments give academic scholars theories to work with. Having meaningful theories to work with will assist the project management community in implementing new knowledge and techniques in the field. Project management should strengthen its philosophical foundations to include ideas in the sociological, cultural, political, and spiritual realms. The project management community should be engaged in adapting new ideas and changes and look at how social networks and collaborative thinking work in project management.

- From the practice standpoint, project management will be the accepted way of getting work done in a flexible, outsourced, and projectized environment. Eventually, project management will become commonplace or the "norm" in organizations. There will be more acceptance and recognition for the project management discipline. Organizations will come to the realization that project management is directly related to achieving strategic goals. More effort and emphasis will be placed on the successful management of the portfolio of projects as opposed to individual projects one at a time. This will require better use of OB/HRM and communications within the organization. Project management will provide the means for organizations to implement continual improvement. Project management is the current wave of global business, and project management would come to be a discipline and a profession of prestige in the business world.

- Eventually, project management will be an exciting knowledge area with solid theory where practitioners and academics can meet, where theory and practice can be co-produced. It is important to note that project management is no longer merely a practice to plan, schedule, and execute projects effectively, but it is an academic field and one of the key management disciplines that consist of both practical/empirical research and theoretical research based on solid academic theory and foundations. Scholars and practitioners in the project management community may need to further justify, defend, and promote project management as an academic discipline by being more vigilant of other allied disciplines and continue to spread understanding of project management not only within the project management domain but also to other management fields. However, there are some positive signs: More publications of project management research in allied disciplines, more papers are being recognized and published in mainstream management journals, and the trends of future research are strong and healthy based on our analysis.

CHAPTER 1

Introduction

1.1 Problem Statement

Project management has been practiced for thousands of years as evidenced by the pyramids, the Great Wall of China, Greek architecture, and Roman roads and viaducts. It has been about half a century since organizations started to apply systematic project management tools and techniques to complex projects. In the 1950s, the U.S. Navy employed modern project management techniques in its Polaris project, and DuPont employed similar tools in its engineering and construction projects. During the 1960s and 1970s, the U.S. Department of Defense, NASA, and large engineering and construction companies utilized project management principles, methodologies, and tools to manage large-budget, schedule-driven projects. In the 1980s, manufacturing and software development sectors started to adopt and implement sophisticated project management practices. By the 1990s, project management theories, tools, and techniques were being widely adopted by different industries and organizations.

Researchers and practitioners adapted different academic disciplines to contribute to the body of knowledge in project management. Network scheduling techniques (CPM/PERT, simulation), decision making tools (decision trees, analytical hierarchy process), and resource allocation and optimization approaches (linear programming and systems dynamics) come from the management science discipline. Network analysis and expert witnesses concerning float often became crucial factors in legal actions over project delays and cost overruns. Recent organizational dynamics theories have provided insights, and the benefits to project-driven organizations have been recognized. Supply chain management (logistics) and business process outsourcing also impacted organizational effectiveness and attitudes on managing projects. Organizational behavior and development issues, such as motivation, leadership, and conflict resolution, influenced and are being influenced by project management.

Allied disciplines have influenced project management and in return it influenced them. Therefore, innovative theories, trends and challenges learned from investigating allied disciplines of project management could have important implications and applications on the future of project management.

1.2 Research Questions

To clarify the importance of project management as a theoretical and practical management discipline, we addressed the following questions given by the Project Management Institute (PMI):

- What future trends in the allied disciplines might significantly impact project management?
- How would the allied disciplines' trends change project management?
- How would project managers have to change their mindset because of the allied disciplines' trends impact?
- How do we behave proactively to meet challenges of allied disciplines' trends?

1.3 Study Design and Measures

The research team conducted extensive literature reviews, an extensive survey, interviews, and discussions with leading project management theorists, researchers and practitioners to identify the emerging trends and challenges of project management. This report addresses trends in the allied disciplines and their expected future, organizational changes, cultural implications and challenges, all of which have important potential impact on the future of project management.

1.4 Data Collection and Analysis

Appropriate data collection methods and analysis procedures were applied throughout this research. The results of the research contribute to the progress of the project management community and motivate it to assess, rethink and enhance the project management discipline.

Data collection involved three steps:
- Extensive literature review
  - We identified eight allied disciplines that have potential impact on project management.

- We selected 18 top management journals and analyzed articles that addressed project management research in the eight allied disciplines.
- Survey design and administration
  - We designed and administered a survey to the project management community to collect data about the availability of knowledge and information regarding the allied disciplines and their impact on project management by decade (1960s, 1970s, etc.). We also collected data on thoughts and opinions of project management impact, trends and future.
- Interviews with project management scholars and practitioners
  - We conducted face-to-face and telephone, in-depth interviews with selected allied disciplines' researchers and project management experts to identify the trends, challenges, and future of the project management discipline.

Data analysis involved two steps:
- Analysis of literature and survey data included a variety of widely accepted social sciences practices including decision sciences, organizational behavior, human resources management, information technology applications, and technology management.
- Analysis of thoughts collected in the survey of the project management community and in-depth interviews identified trends, obstacles, and the future of project management and the impact of allied disciplines on it.

1.5 Relationships Sought and Study Approach
The research team identified eight allied disciplines:
1. Operations Research/Decision Sciences/Operation Management/Supply Chain Management (OR/DS/OM/SCM)
2. Organizational Behavior/Human Resources Management (OB/HRM)
3. Information Technology/Information Systems (IT/IS)
4. Technology Applications/Innovation/New Product Development/Research and Development (TECH/INNOV/NPD/R&D)
5. Engineering and Construction/Contracts/Legal Aspects/Expert Witness (EC/CONTRACT/LEGAL)
6. Strategy/Integration/Portfolio Management/Value of Project Management and Marketing (STRATEGY/PPM)
7. Performance Management/Earned Value Management/Project Finance and Accounting (PERFORMANCE/EVM)
8. Quality Management/Six Sigma/Process Improvement (QM/6SIGMA/PI)

Based on these disciplines, we were able to analyze past, current and future trends of the allied disciplines.

- **Find and plot the current and future availability-impact relationships with allied disciplines related to project management.** For each allied discipline, we developed a 2×2 matrix: On the horizontal (X) axis, we showed the availability of knowledge and information, and on the vertical (Y) axis, we showed the impact of each allied discipline on project management. The results were plotted for each allied discipline.
- **Identify how the allied disciplines' trends change project management.** Project management practitioners were surveyed on project management trends and predictions. Project management researchers were surveyed as well.
- **Conduct a structured survey of how the project management community needs to look forward at the allied disciplines' trends, and how that will improve the understanding of what kind of mindset project managers should have or develop.** Based on extensive analysis of the survey results of the project management community and evaluation of experts' subjective judgment, we identified how the project management community as a whole could respond and meet the opportunities and challenges that lie ahead in the future. The research team incorporated all the reviews and recommendations and compiled proactive response strategies toward these macro trends that are happening now and expected to happen in the future.

1.6 Research Challenges

- Learning from other similar emerging disciplines.
  - Understanding how other disciplines have impacted project management principles, applications and techniques; what impact did project management have on other allied disciplines; and where other disciplines stand right now as a result of that. For example, information technology/information systems (IT/IS) also struggled to become academic disciplines because they were widely regarded as a practice and not an academic discipline. The impact that IT/IS has received from other disciplines as well as IT/IS influence on other disciplines and related challenges and obstacles would be an interesting way to learn from a relatively young and promising discipline.
- Identifying specifics of impact on project management.
  - Looking into the future and identifying specifics are difficult tasks to accomplish. Since other disciplines are not necessarily familiar with the definition or principles of "project management," deriving valuable information from expert panels

is a challenge. The key is being open-minded to the potential impact of other allied disciplines on project management and vice versa. The research team did not try to judge other experts' opinions but rather collected, categorized, and evaluated these opinions to incorporate both the positive and negative impact on project management.

- Seeking statistical relationships between project management and allied disciplines.
  - Identifying the possible impact of allied disciplines on project management was mainly accomplished by qualitative and subjective approaches rather than a quantitative approach. As the first study ever to determine the potential impact of allied disciplines on project management, the research team focused on conceptual, macro, qualitative relationships rather than statistical relationships. At this point, trying to figure out statistically valid information is relatively meaningless. It is more important to find out what factors have influenced project management and what areas or disciplines project management will contribute to in the future. The primary reason why the research team collected data from the project management community was to provide beneficial and valuable information rather than sending out quick surveys to an unidentified, untargeted population and analyzing the survey data.

1.7 Summary

In today's dynamic and competitive business world, cutting-edge research is needed to integrate project management with allied disciplines to maximize their synergistic effects. The goal of this research is to identify the impact on project management of allied disciplines and explore innovative project management theories, new trends and challenges to manage projects effectively. The investigators explored the full range of technical and organizational dynamics of project management, contributing new insights to its theory and practice. This will help in guiding future research and achieving organizational and strategic goals of the project management community.

CHAPTER 2

Project Management Research Trends of Allied Disciplines

2.1 Introduction

This chapter looks at project management from the perspective of its relationship to allied disciplines in the management field. By exploring, identifying, and classifying management journal articles of project management allied disciplines, the evolution and trends of project management research are revealed. This chapter specifically investigates research in the allied disciplines from the management academy's viewpoint, instead of looking at project management research trends from the project management community's perspective. The goal of this research is to better understand project management from the management world and argues that project management is a legitimate academic discipline by reviewing research trends of its allied disciplines. To thoroughly investigate project management research in the allied disciplines, it is necessary to review major journal publications in the management and business fields. Since the management and business fields are very broad, this research identified and defined eight different categories of allied disciplines in project management. Then, we selected 18 top business and management academic journals that published articles related to project management to review and categorize journal articles into these eight different areas. By chronologically analyzing and categorizing more than 500 journal articles from the 18 journals in the business and management fields published from the 1950s to the summer of 2007, this study analyzes publications trends of different domains (operations research (OR) vs. organizational behavior (OB) vs. practitioner-oriented) as well as different journals and predicts the future of project management as an academic discipline in the mainstream management research.

2.2 Origin of Project Management

As mentioned earlier, project management has been practiced for thousands of years. In the 1930s, construction project planning, controlling and coordination of six general contractors were required for the Hoover Dam project. In the 1940s, project management techniques were applied to the Manhattan project. In the 1950s, the U.S. Navy employed modern project management methodologies in its Polaris project, and DuPont employed similar tools in its engineering and construction projects. During the 1960s and 1970s, the U.S. Department of Defense, NASA and large engineering and construction companies utilized project management principles and tools to manage large budget, schedule-driven projects. It has been about a half a century since organizations started applying systematic project management tools and techniques to complex projects. During that time, researchers and practitioners conducted theoretical research and initiated discussions related to project management organizational structures, tools, techniques and principles.

Project management as a discipline has evolved from three very different management fields. One was from management science (MS) and operations research (OR) applications where researchers are interested in quantitative formulation, modeling, analysis, and applications. Introduction of the critical path method (CPM) and program evaluation and review technique (PERT), as extensions of OR applications in the 1950s, are good examples. Project management research related to MS/OR applications during the 1950s and 1960s included linear programming (Charnes & Cooper, 1957), economic lot scheduling (Rogers, 1958), production and inventory control (Schussel & Price, 1970; Zangill, 1966), CPM computations and applications (Crowston & Thompson, 1967), and decision making applications (Kunreuther, 1969).

Organizational behavioral (OB) science and practice-oriented management were two other management entities that showed great interest in project management. From the late 1950s to the 1960s, *Harvard Business Review* (practice-oriented) and *Academy of Management Journal* (OB) published numerous articles related to project management discussing the project manager (Gaddis, 1959), PERT applications (Miller, 1962), research and development (R&D) project applications (Roman, 1964), project organization (Middleton, 1967), project control (Howell, 1968) and project leadership (Hodgetts, 1968). It is important to note that even in the late 1960s organizational scientists struggled to understand the ambiguous roles, responsibilities, and authorities of project management (Goodman, 1967).

2.3 Project Management Research in the Management Field

There has been a long debate within the management education community as to whether "project management" is a practice or an academic discipline. In the engineering side of the world where the tools and techniques of project management have been applied and implemented successfully, the answer to this question is yes, it is an academic discipline. The civil engineering field has construction engineering and management disciplines where students learn and implement planning, managing, and controlling engineering construction projects. The industrial engineering field applies quantitative methods to manufacturing systems analysis and production planning and scheduling to achieve effective productivity. However, when it comes to the business and management field, business scholars appear puzzled and unconvinced of the notion that project management is an academic discipline. The origin, history, and evolution of project management and its academic background, foundations, and underlying theory have been debated and studied only to a limited extent from the management field's academic perspective and supporting literatures are greatly lacking. There has been some study among project management researchers to identify and rethink project management (Winter & Smith, 2006), but the summary was conceptual in nature, and the research failed to transfer the message outside of the project management field to the broader management academic audience.

This study investigates project management research from the perspective of its relationship to allied disciplines in the management field. By exploring, identifying and classifying top management journal articles related to project management research in its allied disciplines, the origin, evolution and trends of project management research in the management field are revealed. This study specifically investigates project management research in allied disciplines from the management academy's perspective by not observing project management research trends from the perspective of the project management community. The goal of this research is to better understand project management from the perspective of the management world and the trends of specific disciplines and to provide compelling arguments that project management is a legitimate academic discipline.

2.4 Previous Research on Analyzing Publication Trends

For the purpose of this study, we conducted extensive literature reviews and categorized previous research on analyzing publication trends into three major domains: (1) operations research/management science/production and operations management (OR/MS/POM); (2) technology management and entrepreneurship, and information technology/information systems (IT/IS); and (3) project management and construction management.

2.4.1 Operations Research, Management Science, and Production and Operations Management

Reisman and Kirschnick (1994) investigated U.S. flagship OR/MS journals over a 30-year period. They specifically analyzed the key OR/MS journals, *Operations Research, Management Science* and *Interfaces*, all published by INFORMS. One of their major findings was a devolution or natural drift toward "professional regression where a small professional elite core maintains intellectual control over a much wider jurisdiction" (Abbot, 1988; Reisman & Kirschnick, 1994). Ormerod and Kiossis (1997) reviewed four journals based in the United Kingdom/Europe: *Journal of the Operational Research Society, OMEGA, OR Insight* and *European Journal of Operational Research*. They categorized the journal articles into "theory" and "applications" for in-depth analysis. Their study found that most journal papers were theoretical in nature, and practical applications of OR/MS for practitioners were limited and declining. Corbett and Van Wassenhove (1993) analyzed the trends of operations research in the United Kingdom and highlighted the development of soft OR and the governmental pressure for assessing research quality of OR applications. Barman, Tersine, and Buckley (1991) and Barman, Hanna, and LaForge (2001) reviewed the perceived relevance and quality of production and operations management (POM) journals by academicians. Soteriou, Hadjinicola, and Patsia (1999) looked at the POM journals from the European perspective, and Vokurka (1996) analyzed the journals using journal citation analysis.

Goh, Holsapple, Johnson, and Tanner (1997) conducted periodical citation analysis of three prominent POM journals and analyzed the articles by using four different dimensions: breadth, consistency, trend and intensity of recognition. Prasad and Babbar (2000) reviewed literature on international operations management from 28 leading operations management, international business and management journals over a 10 year timeframe. They found that international operations management research provided economic benefits to firms. They also suggested expanding research and application of international operations management to nonprofit organization.

Keefer, Kirkwood, and Corner (2004) analyzed trends in decision analysis applications by looking at top English-language operations research and related journals. They found that the overall rate of publication in applications of decision analysis increased from the 1970s to the 1990s, and the research covered a wide spectrum ranging from private and public sectors to strategic and tactical decisions. They also suggested future needs for advancing decision analysis practice. Recently, Olson (2005) analyzed journals in the operations management field and related disciplines. She conducted two surveys (in 2000 and 2002) of faculty members at top 25 U.S. business schools, obtained quality ratings and rankings of 39 journals, computed five-year impact factors for 29 of these journals, and developed a ranking based on these impact factors. She found evidence of some change in journal quality ratings over the two-year period, although these ratings were more consistent than ratings reported in citation studies.

2.4.2 Technology Management, Entrepreneurship and IT/IS

Reisman (1994) reviewed the last 40 years of the technology management discipline and predicted the future of technology management. He predicted that concerns for the environment, innovation of small- and medium-sized corporations in process and product will lead to new areas of research, and in particular, mentioned that academics should view technology management with flexibility rather than as a fixed phenomenon and allow for inputs from nontraditional fields of practice. He emphasized the importance of bringing practical real-world problems into both classroom settings and research.

Liao (2005) surveyed technology management development using a literature review and classification of articles. Based on the 546 articles he reviewed, Liao categorized technology management into eight areas: (1) technology management framework, (2) general and policy research, (3) information systems, (4) information and communication technology, (5) artificial intelligence/expert systems, (6) database technology, (7) modeling, and (8) statistics methodology. Science Citation Index from Thomson ISI and the Emerald Group Publishing's Index were used as a basis to characterize and analyze the development and evolution of *Technovation* (Merino, Pereira do Carmo, & Alvarez, 2006). Linton and Thongpapanl (2004) conducted a citation analysis of 10 leading technology and innovation management (TIM) specialty journals. They found that TIM journals have specific concentrated areas in addition to traditional management disciplines. More recently, Linton (2006) developed a modified impact factor (MIF) to analyze TIM journals.

In the *Academy of Management Journal,* Ireland, Reutzel, and Webb (2005) reported on what has been published, and what might the future hold for entrepreneurship research. Ireland et al. (2005) categorized focal areas of entrepreneurship into seven areas: (1) small business, (2) institutional entrepreneurship, (3) international entrepreneurship, (4) corporate entrepreneurship, (5) initial public offerings, (6) individuals or entrepreneurs, and (7) new ventures. Their work suggested that there is large progress in entrepreneurship research and concluded that the research has positive trends in the future.

Lee, Gosain, and Im (1999) investigated the evolution of information systems (IS) themes and differences between research and practice. *Information & Management* (I&M) journal profiled research published in I&M for 13 years (Palvia, Pinjain, & Sibley, 2007). The study reported that IS research is dominated by U.S.-based universities but international researchers are catching up, and survey methodology is still the most popular research methodology. The paper concluded that the trends in IS research are promising.

2.4.3 Project Management and Construction Management

In project management, Betts and Lansley (1995) investigated papers published in *International Journal of Project Management* for the first 10 years and found that papers mainly reviewed practical experience and literature and contributed to interesting insights and new tools and techniques. The construction industry remained predominant followed by the service sector (Themistocleous & Wearne, 2000). In terms of theory building and the theoretical basis of project management, there was large room for improvement. Their paper concluded that the future development of project management as a discipline should be done by building and testing different research models so that a theory of project management may emerge. Crawford, Pollack, and England (2006) analyzed the trends of emphasis within project management literature by investigating two flagship project management journals: *Project Management Journal* and *International Journal of Project Management.* The authors found a reduction in focus on interpersonal issues and quality management and increased research in project evaluation, improvement, and strategic alignment.

In construction management, historical background and perspectives on engineering and construction research trends were examined by reviewing articles published in *Journal of Construction Engineering and Management* (JCEM) for 18 years (Abudayyeh, Dibert-DeYoung, & Jaselskis, 2004). The study found an increasing number of international submissions to the JCEM and suggested increasing research collaboration between industry and academia, and between government and academia. The paper emphasized practical research and concluded with a note that without industry's input and collaboration, advancement of construction management research would be isolated and alienated.

2.5 Research Approach

To thoroughly investigate project management research in allied disciplines, we reviewed major journal publications from the management and business fields. Respected journals in the management community including The Institute for Operations Research and the Management Sciences (INFORMS), Academy of Management (AOM), Institute of Electrical and Electronics Engineers (IEEE) and others were analyzed in detail. Since the management and business fields are very broad, we identified and defined eight different categories of project management allied disciplines. Then, we selected 18 top business and management academic journals that published articles related to project management to review and categorize journal articles into these eight different areas. By chronologically analyzing and categorizing more than 500 journal articles from the 18 top journals in the management and business fields published between the 1950s and the summer of 2007, this study analyzed publications trends of different domains (OR vs. OB vs. practitioner) in different journals. This study helps us better understand the evolution of project management as a field and discipline, and allows us to provide suggestions for future project management research opportunities.

2.5.1 Top Management Journals

Business schools appear to be obsessed with their annual rankings measured by different entities such as *Business Week, Wall Street Journal, U.S. News and World Report* and *Financial Times*. For the *Financial Times*, one of the criteria to rank a business school is to look at faculty publications in their predefined top 40 journals (FT40). This study investigated journal articles from the FT40 (including publications from INFORMS and AOM), and *IEEE Transactions on Engineering Management* as a primary data set. One can argue that the FT40 list is a specific list solely used to rank business schools in the world and may not represent management research properly. We used the FT40 list as a starting point. Rather than trying to define top journals in their represented fields in management, we thought that reviewing the articles from this list would give us more legitimacy and a firm ground for project management research and its relationship to allied disciplines. As a result, we have identified the following 18 top academic mainstream research journals that represent the fields of operations research, management science, organizational behavior, and practice:

Academy of Management
1. *AOM Perspectives/Executives* (AMP)
2. *AOM Journal* (AMJ)
3. *AOM Review* (AMR)

INFORMS
4. *Operations Research* (OR)
5. *Management Science* (MS)
6. *Organization Science* (OS)
7. *Information Systems Research* (ISR)
8. *Interfaces* (INTFCS)

Practitioner
9. *Harvard Business Review* (HBR)
10. *California Management Review* (CMR)
11. *Sloan Management Review* (SMR)
12. *Long Range Planning* (LRP)

IEEE Engineering Management Society
13. *IEEE Transactions of Engineering Management* (IEEE-TEM)

Other Journals from FT40
14. *Journal of Operations Management* (JOM)
15. *MIS Quarterly* (MISQ)
16. *Strategic Management Journal* (SMJ)
17. *Administrative Science Quarterly* (ASQ)
18. *Journal of Small Business* (JSB)

It can be argued that project management is a focused field and there are specific journals dedicated to project management research, such as *Project Management Journal, International Journal of Project Management,* and the new *International Journal of Managing Projects in Business,* as well as construction management related journals, such as *Journal of Construction Engineering and Management* and *Journal of Management in Engineering* published by the American Society of Civil Engineers, and *Construction Management and Economics* published in the United Kingdom and others. These journals are the flagship journals that represent the project management field, and every article in these journals discusses project management principles, tools, and techniques. The project management community already acknowledges that project management is an academic discipline with practical applications. To establish a strong foundation in the management field, it is essential that we review journal papers that are not published in the project management community research domain but in key management disciplines and analyze the trends of project management research in allied disciplines. Therefore, this study selected the FT40 list as a basis to identify journal articles that are related to project management in their representative management field.

2.5.2 Eight Allied Disciplines

Eight allied disciplines have been identified and defined to incorporate broad research publications in the project management field. We believe that the following eight categories represent the allied disciplines where one can find project management research:

1. **Operations Research/Decision Sciences/Operation Management/Supply Chain Management (OR/DS/OM/SCM)** refers to the discipline associated with quantitative decision analysis and management principles including various optimization tools and techniques, network analysis, resource leveling, simulation, etc.

2. **Organizational Behavior/Human Resources Management (OB/HRM)** refers to the discipline associated with organizational structure, organizational dynamics, motivation, leadership, conflict management, etc.

3. **Information Technology/Information Systems (IT/IS)** refers to the discipline associated with the use of computers and computer systems to process, transmit, store and retrieve information for better management decisions.

4. **Technology Applications/Innovation/New Product Development/ Research and Development (TECH/INNOV/NPD/ R&D)** refers to the discipline associated with the concepts of making innovative and technological improvements and the research and development of entirely new products, services, and processes.

5. **Engineering and Construction/Contracts/Legal Aspects/ Expert Witness (EC/CONTRACT/LEGAL)** refers to the discipline associated with the use and application of a broad range of professional expertise to resolve issues related to engineering and construction, contracts, expert witness and their legal implications.

6. **Strategy/Integration/Portfolio Management/Value of Project Management/Marketing (STRATEGY/PPM)** refers to the concepts of organizing and managing resources to maximize profit, minimize cost and support the overall strategy of the organization.

7. **Performance Management/Earned Value Management/Project Finance and Accounting (PERFORMANCE/EVM)** refers to the concepts and techniques that measure project progress

objectively by combining measurements of technical performance, schedule performance, and cost performance.

8. **Quality Management/Six Sigma/Process Improvement (QM/6SIGMA/PI)** refers to the concepts of improving processes, minimizing defects, and reducing cost by implementing continual improvement principles and specific measures and metrics.

These eight categories were used as the basis for analyzing allied disciplines of project management for this study.

2.6 Journal Publications Trend Analysis

Eighteen journals have been reviewed and analyzed by using EBSCO-host research database. EBSCOhost is popular among libraries, schools, and other institutions and serves thousands of libraries and other institutions with premium content in every subject area. EBSCOhost has archived manuscripts from the very first journal issues going back to the late 1950s.

Papers published in IEEE-TEM were searched by using IEEE Xplore journal database run by Institute of Electrical and Electronics Engineers. It is important to note that IEEE Xplore allows users to search for papers published for the last 20 years only; therefore, for IEEE-TEM papers, we were able to identify papers related to project management research in allied disciplines starting from 1988. We believe that this limitation from IEEE-TEM would not affect the overall analysis of the papers published in project management and its allied disciplines.

The research team applied a broad definition of project management which includes anything that has to do with planning, managing, controlling, and executing projects and resources. The journal papers we analyzed included the papers published up to June 2007. We identified 537 papers published in 18 top management and business journals. Table 2-1 shows the overall distribution of published journal papers that dealt with project management and its allied disciplines (eight categories), and Figure 2-1 shows the distribution of papers for the 18 journals.

IEEE-TEM (18%) had the most papers (the database only allowed us to search papers for the last 20 years and still had the most papers), followed by *Management Science* (17%), *Long Range Planning* (10%) and *Harvard Business Review* (9%). Papers published in these four journals (two journals were practice-oriented journals, and two journals were more theory-oriented journals) added up to 55% of the total papers published in project management allied disciplines. *Interfaces* (6%), *Journal of Operations Management* (6%), *Operations Research* (5%), and *California Management Review* (5%) followed. It is inter-

Rankings	18 Journal List	50–59	60–69	70–79	80–89	90–99	00–07	Total	%
1	IEEE-TEM	0	0	0	3	39	54	96	18%
2	MS	2	8	20	18	16	27	91	17%
3	LRP	0	0	10	17	18	11	56	10%
4	HBR	2	9	8	12	7	10	48	9%
5	INTFCS	0	0	6	13	6	8	33	6%
6	JOM	0	0	0	8	12	13	33	6%
7	AMJ	0	5	8	3	8	8	32	6%
8	OR	1	3	6	3	10	3	26	5%
9	CMR	0	4	3	2	6	10	25	5%
10	MISQ	0	0	1	13	5	1	20	4%
11	AMP	0	0	0	0	9	9	18	3%
12	ISR	0	0	0	0	7	10	17	3%
13	SMR	0	0	4	4	5	0	13	2%
14	AMR	0	0	2	3	2	4	11	2%
15	SMJ	0	0	0	1	4	4	9	2%
16	OS	0	0	0	0	1	4	5	1%
17	ASQ	0	1	1	1	0	0	3	1%
18	JSB	0	0	0	0	1	0	1	0%
	Total	5	30	69	101	156	176	537	100%
	Percentage	1%	6%	13%	19%	29%	33%	100%	

Table 2-1   Trends of Journal Publications of Allied Disciplines in Project Management

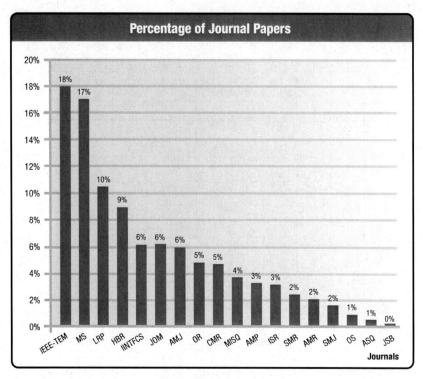

Percentage of Journal Papers

Journals

Figure 2-1   Percentage of Papers Published in 18 Journals

esting to note that the top nine journals published more than 80% of the total papers related to project management. *Strategic Management Journal* (9 papers), *Organization Science* (5 papers), *Administrative Science Quarterly* (3 papers), and *Journal of Small Business* (1 paper) were the four journals that had the least number of papers.

Publications related to project management research in allied disciplines started to increase substantially beginning in the 1980s. In fact, over 80% of the papers were published after 1980. At this time project management principles, tools, and techniques started to gain wide interest among academicians and practitioners. Project management tools and techniques started to be applied beyond large engineering-construction or aerospace-defense projects, and widespread usage of personal computers greatly contributed to the popularity of project management and related research. By the 1990s, project management related papers had appeared in every journal on the list.

Figure 2-2 shows the journal publication trends beginning in 1980. *Academy of Management Review, Information Systems Research, California Management Review, Harvard Business Review, Management Science,* and *IEEE Transactions on Engineering Management* are the key journals that showed an increase in publication ratio of 50% to 100% from the 1990s to the 2000s. Overall, there is a strong positive publications trend of project management related research in all 18 journals.

2.7 Allied Disciplines Trend Analysis

The research team also wanted to learn more about the kind of allied disciplines that covered project management research and further analyze the trends of occurrences of allied disciplines in top management journals using the specified eight categories. Based on the 537 papers that we investigated, we coded each and every paper in up to three categories. For example, let us say that there was a paper titled "Information technology implementation project: measuring performance using earned value management in an R&D organiza-

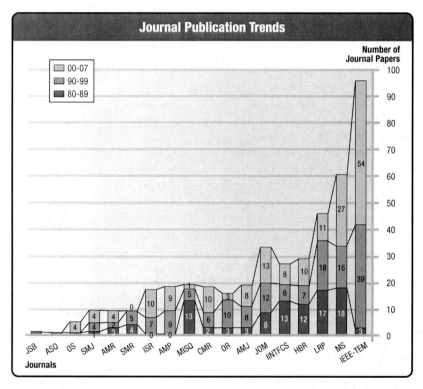

Figure 2-2   Eighteen Journal Publication Trends from 1980 to 2007

tion." Then, we coded the paper as covering IT/IS (IT implementation issues), PERFORMANCE/EVM (project effectiveness measurement using EVM) and TECH/INNOV/NPD/R&D (new product development projects). In other cases, papers were coded for only one or two combined categories. Based on this coding scheme, we identified 980 total occurrences in the 537 papers using the eight disciplines/categories as shown in Table 2-2.

Overall, more papers were being published on project management in the allied disciplines beginning in the 1980s (19%), 1990s (30%), and continuing in the 2000s (31%) showing a greater interest in project management research in the allied disciplines. STRATEGY/PPM (30%) and OR/DS/OM/SCM (23%) were the two primary disciplines that appeared most among the allied disciplines. In particular, the STRATEGY/PPM category was always the most popular subject starting from the 1950s with a strong and continued upward trend in research interest. Scholars and practitioners have a keen interest in applying project management principles, tools, techniques and concepts to organize and manage resources for maximizing profit, minimizing cost and supporting the overall strategy of the organization. Regarding OR/DS/OM/SCM, it is only natural that OR/DS/OM/SCM was ranked highly since project management has strong roots in OR/DS/OM/SCM. The appearance of occurrences in OR/DS/OM/SCM seems to be slowing down from the 2000s and has recently flattened.

In OB/HRM, another major field that has a strong theoretical foundation related to project management, research interests peaked in the 1990s and started to flatten out as well. IT/IS and TECH/INNOV/NPR/R&D showed a steady increase of interest in terms of the number of occurrences in the papers categorized from the 1990s. PERFORMANCE/EVM is the area in which research interest spiked more than 100% from 2000s. However, in terms of overall research interest, the proportion was very small (7%). It could be interpreted that researchers are realizing the benefits of applying and implementing project management concepts and techniques that measure project progress objectively by combining measurements of technical performance, schedule performance and cost performance.

EC/CONTRACT/LEGAL (3%) and QM/6SIGMA/PI (2%) were the two categories that had the least appearance in related publications. It is important to note that if we broaden the journals that we investigated and analyzed, the result could be totally different for these two categories. EC/CONTRACT/LEGAL is probably the most published area in project management among all the allied disciplines if we included the construction engineering management related journals as well as project management focused journals. The

Allied Disciplines	50–59	60–69	70–79	80–89	90–99	00–07	TOTAL	%
OR/DS/OM/SCM	3	20	37	49	65	54	228	23%
OB/HRM	1	5	18	14	46	43	127	13%
IT/IS	2	2	7	22	35	37	105	11%
TECH/INNOV/NPD/R&D	0	1	12	13	39	46	111	11%
EC/CONTRACT/LEGAL	1	4	2	4	10	7	28	3%
STRATEGY/PPM	2	10	48	74	78	83	295	30%
PERFORMANCE/EVM	1	6	10	11	12	28	68	7%
QM/6SIGMA/PI	0	1	2	1	7	7	18	2%
Total	10	49	136	188	292	305	980	100%
Percentage	1%	5%	14%	19%	30%	31%	100%	

Table 2-2   Journal Publications Trends Based on Eight Allied Disciplines

same assumption applies also to QM/6SIGMA/PI category as project management and QM/6SIGMA/PI share many of the key principles, tools, and techniques, and there are plenty of QM dedicated journals.

2.8 Future Project Management Research Trends

Table 2-1 showed detailed distribution by journals and decades. Figure 2-1 showed that the top four journals published more than 50% of the total papers related to project management. Figure 2-2 presented journal publication trends by decade beginning in the 1980s. Figure 2-3 is a bar chart presenting the number of journal publications by decade.

We identified 537 papers from 18 prestigious journals that cover subjects related to project management in the allied disciplines. We conducted a simple linear regression analysis to better understand and possibly extrapolate future trends of project management research publication in top management journals. The analysis result was somewhat surprising in that the R^2 was 0.99 and every decade publications were increasing by approximately 40 (~36.143) papers.

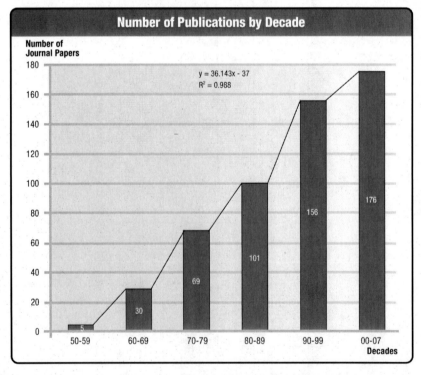

Figure 2-3   Number of Journal Paper Publications by Decade

Regression analysis shows a strong positive upward trend in project management research publications in the allied disciplines.

From the project management community, project management oriented journals including *International Journal of Project Management, Project Management Journal* and *Journal of Construction Engineering and Management* all have had rapid growth in the number of publications. The size and publication frequency of those journals have more than doubled over the last 20 years. A new journal, *International Journal of Managing Projects in Business,* began publication in 2008. Based on our analysis, this same trend also applies to the 18 selected top business and management journals that we analyzed from the perspectives of allied disciplines. It is predicted that more integrated and interdisciplinary project management research will appear in the future. Project management research in three or more combined allied disciplines will be common and new allied disciplines such as politics, social, ethics, sports, events, and entertainment will also adopt project management as one of the major research themes to conduct research related to project management in their disciplines.

2.9 Discussions and Conclusion

Project management is one of the youngest, most vibrant, and most dynamic fields among different management disciplines along with other established business fields such as operations research, organizational behavior, strategy, etc. The roots of modern project management have come from quantitative research in planning-oriented techniques as well as an application of engineering science and optimization theory (Söderlund, 2004). In recent years, research interests in cross-disciplinary studies between project management and allied disciplines have become more popular, as evidenced by increased publications on these integrated subjects in mainstream business and management journals. We have seen an explosion of popularity and strong interest in project management research beginning in the 1980s and the trends are likely to continue in the future. It is important to note that project management is no longer merely a practice to plan, schedule, and execute projects effectively, but it is an academic field and one of the key management disciplines that consist of both practical/empirical research and theoretical research based on solid academic theory and foundations.

It is interesting to look into the history of business and management education in the United Kingdom. Back in the 1960s, the U.K. government offered Oxford and Cambridge money to set up management faculties. Both institutions said that "management" was not a proper discipline so the funds went to London and Manchester instead (private communication with Rodney Turner, 2007). London Business School and Manchester Business School became the beneficiaries of Oxford and Cambridge snobbery (Franks Report, 1963).

In their book *Effective Learning and Teaching in Business and Management*, Macfarlane and Ottewill (2001) noted:

> The derivative and vocational nature of knowledge in business and management has led critics to argue that the study of business is a spurious discipline with a dubious claim to academic legitimacy. (p. 7)

They quoted Bain (1990, p. 13) who quoted a Professor of English who said:

> [B]usiness is educationally suspect because it is not a discipline. . . The syllabus is an agglomeration of several disciplines, and the student may not get an adequate grounding in any of them. The departments tend to be so large and so closely linked to industry that they threaten to be a Trojan horse inside the university. (p. 8)

Furthermore, they quoted O'Hear (1988, p. 14) who claimed:

> Such business and management departments are in fact simply training schools for management, and live off the fruits from other trees of knowledge. While there can be no objection to such schools in their proper place, it is quite unclear why they should exist in universities, or why people working in them should enjoy the specific academic freedom which involves their having tenure. Those who live by the market should die . . . by the market. (p. 8)

Sir George Sayers Bain (1992), past principal of the London Business School (1989–1997) and past President of Queen's University, Belfast (1998–2004), described how the position of management in Britain has changed over the second half of the twentieth century, identified the qualities required for successful managers in the 1990s and beyond, discussed the ways in which managers might acquire these qualities and the role of business schools, companies, and the wider society in this process, and made comments about the role of operational research in the future of management education. He stated:

> Business schools are too functionally fragmented. Too much of their teaching and learning is compartmentalized into distinct disciplines. Students leave business schools thinking that there are accounting problems, finance problems, mar-

keting problems, production problems, and so on. What they find, however, are business problems which involve several of these functional areas and which require managers to manage the interfaces between them . . . business schools concentrated mainly on problem-solving. They did so because problem-solving, to a greater extent than path breaking or implementation, lent itself to quantification and rigorous analysis. In short, it was more 'scientific' or at least more congenial to the academic mind. More recently, business schools have begun to put more emphasis on implementation, but still pay little attention to path breaking. What is now needed is more inter-disciplinary, issue-based, and project-based teaching, a greater stress on learning and less on teaching, and more emphasis on path breaking and implementation, including such process skills as negotiation and team building. In short, business schools need to develop a more balanced relationship between analysis and the more subjective aspects of management. (p. 560)

These quotes basically show that some humanities and social science scholars are still not convinced of management education and research. In the case of project management, the field is more applied and interdisciplinary than other management disciplines, so naturally it is more difficult to justify the field as an academic discipline within the academic management community, and more obstacles lie ahead. However, there are some positive signs: there are more publications on project management research in allied disciplines, more papers are being recognized and published in mainstream management journals, and the trends of future research are strong and healthy based on our analysis.

Scholars and practitioners in the project management community may need to further justify, defend, and promote project management as an academic discipline by being more vigilant of other allied disciplines and continue to spread understanding of project management not only within the project management domain but also to other management fields. The analysis of project management research in the allied disciplines shows strong evidence that this phenomenon is happening now, and we are witnessing that the future has arrived.

CHAPTER 3

Analyzing Project Management Research Trends from Eight Allied Disciplines

3.1 Introduction

Eight allied disciplines that incorporate project management research in their fields have been identified to conduct in-depth trend analysis of project management related research. These eight allied disciplines are:

- Operations Research, Decision Sciences, Operation Management, and Supply Chain Management (OR/DS/OM/SCM)
- Organizational Behavior and Human Resources Management (OB/HRM)
- Information Technology and Information Systems (IT/IS)
- Technology, Innovation, New Product Development, and Research and Development (TECH/INNOV/NPD/R&D)
- Engineering-Construction, Contracts, Legal Aspects, and Expert Witness (EC/CONTRACT/LEGAL)
- Strategy, Integration, Portfolio Management, Value of Project Management, and Marketing (STRATEGY/PPM)
- Performance Management, Earned Value Management, Project Finance, and Accounting (PERFORMANCE/EVM)
- Quality Management, Six Sigma, and Process Improvement (QM/6SIGMA/PI)

It is important to note that we used the broadest definition of "project management" to incorporate papers related to project management research from top management and business journals. We used the definition given by the *PMBOK® Guide* (Project Management Institute, 2004) as a starting point. However, we broadened that definition because scholars, practitioners, and academic and professional societies have different definitions and interpretations of the subject "project management," and it is necessary to take into consideration their viewpoint adequately. For example, in discussing project management, behavioral scientists would think of the matrix organization or emotional intelligence; operational researchers would think of network analysis, queuing theory, or optimal plant design; and strategy scholars would think of strategic alliances among different organizations during project execution. We think that this approach would be an important step in expanding project management research interests to allied disciplines.

Eighteen top management journals have been carefully selected to further analyze project management research trends of the eight allied disciplines and categorized into organizational management, operations research/management science, practitioner-oriented, engineering management, and others:

  Academy of Management (AOM)
  - *AOM Perspectives/Executives* (AMP)
  - *AOM Journal* (AMJ)
  - *AOM Review* (AMR)
- The Institute for Operations Research and The Management Science (INFORMS)
  - *Operations Research* (OR)
  - *Management Science* (MS)
  - *Organization Science* (OS)
  - *Information Systems Research* (ISR)
  - *Interfaces* (INTFCS)
- Practitioners
  - *Harvard Business Review* (HBR)
  - *California Management Review* (CMR)
  - *Sloan Management Review* (SMR)
  - *Long Range Planning* (LRP)
- IEEE Engineering Management Society
  - *IEEE Transactions of Engineering Management* (IEEE TEM)
- Other Journals from FT40
  - *Journal of Operations Management* (JOM)
  - *MIS Quarterly* (MISQ)
  - *Strategic Management Journal* (SMJ)
  - *Administrative Science Quarterly* (ASQ)
  - *Journal of Small Business* (JSB)

By analyzing these key management journals and revealing the trends of project management research in allied disciplines, we could better understand the trends of project management research in allied disciplines as well as the evolution of project management theory and practice over the last 50 years. It also revealed what areas have matured and what areas have potential opportunities to conduct research in the future. It is important to note that the numbers in the tables are occurrences of specific disciplines that have been identified, so the total numbers are different from the actual number of journal papers as many articles discuss more than one area of allied disciplines.

For example, if there was a paper dealing with identifying critical success factors of implementing an enterprise resource planning (ERP) system in a hi-tech manufacturing company, we coded the paper as covering IT/IS (ERP system implementation), OR/DS/MS/SCM (used advanced statistical analysis to identify critical success factors), and TECH/INNV/NPD/R&D (hi-tech manufacturing environment). In other cases, papers were coded for only one or two categories. For any given paper, we limited the coding to a maximum of three allied disciplines. One can argue that evaluating and determining proper codes for these papers could be subjective in nature. We appreciate the concern but in most cases, it is quite clear and obvious as to where those papers belong. There might be a handful of papers to which it could be difficult to assign proper codes. However, since the size of data set is large, we believe that it did not affect the overall trend analysis. Please refer to Appendix A for the entire list of papers and classification codes that we have assigned for every article related to project management research from the top 18 management and business journals.

3.2 Academy of Management

The Academy of Management is a professional association for scholars dedicated to creating and disseminating knowledge about management and organizations. Founded in 1936 by two professors, the AOM is the oldest and largest scholarly management association in the world (AOM, 2007). AOM publishes four journals: *AOM Perspectives* (formerly *AOM Executive*), *AOM Journal*, *AOM Review*, and *AOM Learning & Education* (AMLE). We selected *AOM Perspectives*, *AOM Journal*, and *AOM Review*. AMLE was excluded from this analysis because the journal was first published in 2002, and moreover, there were no papers related to project management as of the summer of 2007.

3.2.1 AOM Perspectives/Executive

"AOM Perspectives is to provide accessible articles about important issues concerning management and business. AMP articles are aimed at the nonspecialist academic reader, not practicing managers, and rely on evidence as opposed to theory or opinion for their arguments. Articles might include reviews of what we already know about particular topics, with an orientation specifically toward practical implications. Descriptive articles might also be relevant if they advance our understanding of business and management practice" (*AOM Perspectives*, 2007). AMP was first published in 1987. This journal used to be called *AOM Executive* and in 2006, the journal was renamed *AOM Perspectives*.

Table 3-1 shows project management research trends in AMP. Project management related research papers in AMP included subjects on virtual teams (Cascio, 2000; Karl, 1999; Malhotra, Majchrzak, & Benson, 2007; Townsend, DeMarie, & Hendrickson, 1998), issues on team-based organizational performance (Cianni & Wnuck, 1997; Forrester & Drexler, 1999; Scott & Einstein, 2001), issues in product development (Jassawalla & Sashittal, 2002; Kessler & Bierly, 2001; Leifer, O'Connor, & Rice, 2001), aligning projects with objectives (Bunch, 2003; Miles, Snow, Mathews, Miles, & Coleman Jr., 1997) and others. Over 90% of the papers were from OB/HRM (75%) and STRATEGY/PPM (15%). This analysis shows that AMP publishes project management research that emphasizes organizational and strategic issues. AMP did not have any project management research papers from the OR/DS/OM/SCM, TECH/INNOV/NPD/

No.	Allied Disciplines	50–59	60–69	70–79	80–89	90–99	00–07	TOTAL	%
1	OR/DS/OM/SCM	X	X	X	X	0	0	0	0%
2	OB/HRM	X	X	X	X	8	7	15	75%
3	IT/IS	X	X	X	X	1	0	1	5%
4	TECH/INNOV/NPD/R&D	X	X	X	X	0	0	0	0%
5	EC/CONTRACT/LEGAL	X	X	X	X	0	0	0	0%
6	STRATEGY/PPM	X	X	X	X	0	3	3	15%
7	PERFORMANCE/EVM	X	X	X	X	0	0	0	0%
8	QM/6SIGMA/PI	X	X	X	X	1	0	1	5%
	TOTAL	X	X	X	X	10	10	20	100%
	PERCENTAGE	X	X	X	X	50%	50%	100%	

Table 3-1   Project Management Research Trends in *Academy of Management Perspectives*

R&D, EC/CONTRACT/LEGAL, and PERFORMANCE/EVM categories.

3.2.2 AOM Journal

Academy of Management Journal publishes "empirical research
that tests, extends, or builds management theory and contributes to
management practice. To be published in AMJ, a manuscript must
make strong empirical and theoretical contributions and highlight
the significance of those contributions to the management field.
Thus, preference is given to submissions that test, extend, or build
strong theoretical frameworks while empirically examining issues
with high importance for management theory and practice. AMJ is
not tied to any particular discipline, level of analysis, or national
context" (Academy of Management Journal, 2007).

As shown in Table 3-2, a total of 50 occurrences of different
allied disciplines appeared in 32 AMJ papers. Approximately 60%
of the articles covered the area of OR/DS/OM/SCM (28%), and OB/
HRM (30%) followed by STRATEGY/PPM (16%) and TECH/
INNOV/NPD/R&D (14%). IT/IS did not appear in AMJ. It seems
that most project management related papers were published
during the 1960s and 1970s (Cook & Granger, 1976; Delionback &
Meinhart, 1968; Dunne, Stahl, & Melhart Jr., 1978; Goodman, 1967;
Roman, 1964; Thamhain & Gemmil, 1974; Wilemon & Cicero,
1970).

In the 1980s, the number of project management papers published in AMJ declined by one-third (there were only three papers
in the 1980s), and the amount of papers published during the 1990s
began to increase again. The *International Journal of Project Man-*

No.	Allied Disciplines	50–59	60–69	70–79	80–89	90–99	00–07	TOTAL	%
1	OR/DS/OM/SCM	0	3	3	1	3	4	14	28%
2	OB/HRM	0	1	4	2	5	3	15	30%
3	IT/IS	0	0	0	0	0	0	0	0%
4	TECH/INNOV/NPD/R&D	0	1	0	1	2	3	7	14%
5	EC/CONTRACT/LEGAL	0	3	0	0	0	1	4	8%
6	STRATEGY/PPM	0	0	7	1	0	0	8	16%
7	PERFORMANCE/EVM	0	0	1	0	0	0	1	2%
8	QM/6SIGMA/PI	0	0	0	0	1	0	1	2%
	TOTAL	0	8	15	5	11	11	50	100%
	PERCENTAGE	0%	16%	30%	10%	22%	22%	100%	

Table 3-2   Project Management Research Trends in *Academy
of Management Journal*

agement was first published in the 1980s, and organizations started to recognize the benefits of applying project management tools and techniques to complex projects, however, AMJ showed little interest in project management research. The three disciplines that increased in publication beginning from the 1980s were OR/DS/OM/SCM (28%), OB/HRM (30%), and TECH/INNOV/NPD/R&D (14%).

3.2.3 AOM Review

Academy of Management Review publishes "new theoretical insights that advance our understanding of management and organizations. AMR is receptive to a variety of perspectives, including those seeking to improve the effectiveness of, as well as those critical of, management and organizations. The contributions of AMR articles often are grounded in "normal science disciplines" of economics, psychology, sociology, or social psychology as well as nontraditional perspectives, such as the humanities" (*Academy of Management Review*, 2007).

There were 24 occurrences from 11 papers. AMR started to publish more project management related papers during the 2000s. Similar to AMJ, subjects related to OR/DS/OM/SCM (29%), OB/HRM (25%), and STRATEGY/PPM (21%) were the three allied disciplines that encompassed 75% of the occurrences. There were no papers related to EC/CONTRACT/LEGAL and QM/6SIGMA/PI.

Most papers dealt with two or more allied disciplines that are discussed together. There papers covered three different areas: organizational alignment and strategy (Gottschalg & Zollo, 2007), NPD and strategic alliances (Gerwin, 2004), and cost and resource allocation (Northcraft & Wolf, 1984). Table 3-3 shows project management research trends in *Academy of Management Review*.

3.2.4 Project Management Research Trends in Academy of Management Journals

To better analyze and understand the overall trends of project management research from the Academy of Management perspective, occurrences of allied disciplines in the three journals were combined. Table 3-4 shows the trends of project management research in AOM journals. Overall, project management research in allied disciplines in AOM journals has been increasing over the last 40 years, except during the 1980s (27%) where there was a downturn. OB/HRM (38%) and OR/DS/OM/SCM (22%) were the two main areas that had the most articles followed by STRATEGY/PPM (17%) and TECH/INNOV/NPR/R&D (10%).

Figure 3-1 depicts trends of AOM journals publication of project management research from the four top allied disciplines.

No.	Allied Disciplines	50–59	60–69	70–79	80–89	90–99	00–07	TOTAL	%
1	OR/DS/OM/SCM	X	X	1	2	1	3	7	29%
2	OB/HRM	X	X	1	1	2	2	6	25%
3	IT/IS	X	X	0	1	0	0	1	4%
4	TECH/INNOV/NPD/R&D	X	X	0	0	1	1	2	8%
5	EC/CONTRACT/LEGAL	X	X	0	0	0	0	0	0%
6	STRATEGY/PPM	X	X	2	2	0	1	5	21%
7	PERFORMANCE/EVM	X	X	0	1	0	2	3	13%
8	QM/6SIGMA/PI	X	X	0	0	0	0	0	0%
	TOTAL	X	X	4	7	4	9	24	100%
	PERCENTAGE	0%	0%	17%	29%	17%	38%	100%	

Table 3-3 Project Management Research Trends in *Academy of Management Review*

No.	Allied Disciplines	50–59	60–69	70–79	80–89	90–99	00–07	TOTAL	%
1	OR/DS/OM/SCM	0	3	4	3	4	7	21	22%
2	OB/HRM	0	1	5	3	15	12	6	38%
3	IT/IS	0	0	0	1	1	0	2	2%
4	TECH/INNOV/NPD/R&D	0	1	0	1	3	4	9	10%
5	EC/CONTRACT/LEGAL	0	3	0	0	0	1	4	4%
6	STRATEGY/PPM	0	0	9	3	0	4	16	17%
7	PERFORMANCE/EVM	0	0	1	1	0	2	4	4%
8	QM/6SIGMA/PI	0	0	0	0	2	0	2	2%
	TOTAL	0	8	19	12	25	30	94	100%
	PERCENTAGE	0%	9%	20%	13%	27%	32%	100%	

Table 3-4 Project Management Research Trends in AOM Journals

3.3 INFORMS

The Institute for Operations Research and the Management Sciences (INFORMS) is "the largest professional society in the world for professionals in the field of operations research (OR). It was established in 1995 with the merger of the Operations Research Society of America (ORSA) and The Institute of Management Sciences (TIMS). The society serves the scientific and professional needs of OR educators, investigators, scientists, students, managers, and consultants, as well as the organizations they serve, by such services as publishing 12 scholarly journals that describe the latest OR methods and applications and a membership magazine with news from across the

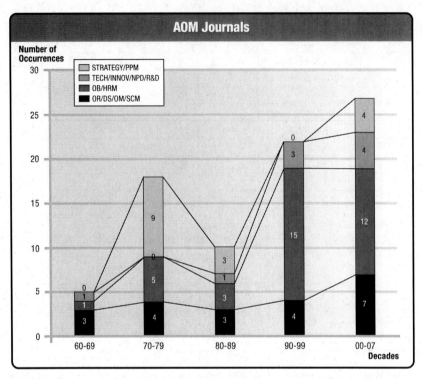

Figure 3-1   Project Management Research Trends in AOM
Journals

profession. The society organizes national and international conferences for academics and professionals, as well as members of the
society's special interest groups. The institute serves as a focal point
for OR professionals, permitting them to communicate with each
other and reach out to other professional societies, as well as the
varied clientele of the profession's research and practice"
(INFORMS, 2007).

From the 12 scholarly journals published by INFORMS, we
selected five journals in their representative fields: *Interfaces* (practice-oriented), *Operations Research, Management Science, Organization Science*, and *Information Systems Research*.

3.3.1 *Interfaces*

Interfaces is dedicated to "improving the practical application
of OR/MS to decisions and policies in today's organizations and
industries. Each article provides details of the completed application,
along with the results and impact on the organization. *Interfaces*
seeks to improve communication between managers and profession-

als in OR/MS and to inform the academic community about practice. The most appropriate papers are descriptions of the practice and implementation of OR/MS in commerce, industry, government, or education" (*Interfaces*, 2007).

Most papers related to project management in *Interfaces* were published in the 1980s and were related to computer applications (Hoffman, 1982; Maxfield, 1981; Vazsonyi, 1982; Wasin & Assad, 1988). Publication of papers declined during the 1990s but it is now starting to slowly catch up again in terms of project management research. Table 3-5 shows that OR/DS/OM/SCM (38%) and STRATEGY/PPM (37%) were the two most published areas of project management related research. This is explained by the fact that the goals and objectives of *Interfaces* are providing practical applications to practitioners and educators and the fact that *Interfaces* is part of INFORMS journals where the focus is on OR/MS issues. There were no articles related to EC/CONTRACT/LEGAL.

3.3.2 *Operations Research*

Operations Research offers a "balance of well-written articles that span the wide array of creative activities in OR. Areas of concentration include: computing and decision technologies; decision analysis; environment, energy, and natural resources; financial engineering; manufacturing, service, and supply chain operations; marketing science; military and homeland security; optimization; policy modeling and public sector OR; revenue management; simulation; stochastic models; telecommunications and networking; and transportation" (*Operations Research*, 2007).

No.	Allied Disciplines	50–59	60–69	70–79	80–89	90–99	00–07	TOTAL	%
1	OR/DS/OM/SCM	X	X	6	9	3	7	25	38%
2	OB/HRM	X	X	1	2	1	0	4	6%
3	IT/IS	X	X	0	2	1	0	3	5%
4	TECH/INNOV/NPD/R&D	X	X	1	1	2	0	4	6%
5	EC/CONTRACT/LEGAL	X	X	0	0	0	0	0	0%
6	STRATEGY/PPM	X	X	4	9	5	6	24	37%
7	PERFORMANCE/EVM	X	X	1	0	0	1	2	3%
8	QM/6SIGMA/PI	X	X	1	0	1	1	3	5%
	TOTAL	X	X	14	23	13	15	65	100%
	PERCENTAGE	0%	0%	22%	35%	20%	23%	100%	

Table 3-5   Project Management Research Trends in *Interfaces*

Table 3-6 represents project management research trends of *Operations Research*. Project management research was most active during the 1990s and then declined sharply in the 2000s. This trend is explained by the phenomenon that project management research evolved from the traditional OR/MS applications in the 1980s and 1990s to managerial/organizational/behavioral/philosophical aspects in the 2000s. In fact, 70% of the occurrences came from two areas: OR/DS/OM/SCM (40%) and STRATEGY/PPM (30%). In contrast, IT/IS (7%), QM/6SIGMA/PI (5%), PERFORMANCE/EVM (5%), and TECH/INNOV/NPD/R&D (2%) combined made up only 19% of the paper subject occurrences. It is also interesting to note that several articles from the 2000s dealt with risk and uncertainty management (Dillon, Paté-Cornell, & Guikema, 2003; Gustafsson & Salo, 2005; Gutierrez & Paul, 2000), highlighting that the topic and importance of risk management is starting to gain strong interest from academia and practice. There were no occurrences from OB/HRM, probably because *Operations Research* publishes papers mainly with strong quantitative analysis.

3.3.3 *Management Science*

Management Science is a "scholarly journal published to scientifically address the problems, interests, and concerns of managers. The journal promotes the science of managing private and public sector enterprises through publication of theoretical, computational, and empirical research that draws on a wide range of management subdisciplines, including accounting, business strategy, decision analysis, finance, information systems, marketing, operations management, operations research, organizational behavior, and product/

No.	Allied Disciplines	50–59	60–69	70–79	80–89	90–99	00–07	TOTAL	%
1	OR/DS/OM/SCM	1	3	6	3	8	3	24	40%
2	OB/HRM	0	0	0	0	0	0	0	0%
3	IT/IS	0	0	1	2	0	1	4	7%
4	TECH/INNOV/NPD/R&D	0	0	0	0	0	1	1	2%
5	EC/CONTRACT/LEGAL	1	1	1	1	2	1	7	12%
6	STRATEGY/PPM	0	2	3	3	9	1	18	30%
7	PERFORMANCE/EVM	0	1	0	0	2	0	3	5%
8	QM/6SIGMA/PI	0	1	1	0	1	0	3	5%
	TOTAL	2	8	12	9	22	7	60	100%
	PERCENTAGE	3%	13%	20%	15%	37%	12%	100%	

Table 3-6　Project Management Research Trends in *Operations Research*

technology management" (*Management Science*, 2007). Table 3-7 represents project management research trends in *Management Science*.

Management Science had the most occurrences of project management allied disciplines in its published papers among the 18 top management journals. Project management research in *Management Science* reached a peak during the 1970s (24%), then started to decline during the 1980s (20%) and 1990s (18%), and is showing renewal of interest in the 2000s (29%). Many papers published in the 2000s discussed three different categories of allied disciplines which shows increasing trends in interdisciplinary research in project management (Butler, Morrice, & Mullarkey, 2001; Haas, 2006; Mihm, Loch, & Huchzermeier, 2003; Mitchell &Nault, 2007; Santiago and Vakili, 2005; Shenhar, 2001; Sivaramakrishnan & Gopal, 2003; Szmerekovsky, 2005; Vanhoucke & Demeulemeester, 2001). Similar to *Operations Research*, OR/DS/OM/SCM (29%) and STRATEGY/PPM (34%) were the areas that made up more than 60% of the publications' subject occurrences while OB/HRM (6%) and EC/CONTRACT/LEGAL (3%) were the areas that had the lowest interest. There were no occurrences in papers in the area of QM/6SIGMA/PI.

3.3.4 *Organization Science*

Organization Science is "ranked among the top journals in management and is widely recognized in the fields of strategy, management, and organization theory. *Organization Science* provides one umbrella for the publication of research from all over the world in fields such as organization theory, strategic management, sociology,

No.	Allied Disciplines	50–59	60–69	70–79	80–89	90–99	00–07	TOTAL	%
1	OR/DS/OM/SCM	1	7	17	11	10	14	60	29%
2	OB/HRM	0	2	3	0	4	3	12	6%
3	IT/IS	2	2	3	2	6	7	22	11%
4	TECH/INNOV/NPD/R&D	0	1	2	6	1	7	17	8%
5	EC/CONTRACT/LEGAL	0	0	1	1	2	3	7	3%
6	STRATEGY/PPM	1	2	16	18	12	21	70	34%
7	PERFORMANCE/EVM	1	1	7	3	2	6	20	10%
8	QM/6SIGMA/PI	0	0	0	0	0	0	0	0%
	TOTAL	5	15	49	41	37	61	208	100%
	PERCENTAGE	2%	7%	24%	20%	18%	29%	100%	

Table 3-7   Project Management Research Trends in *Management Science*

economics, political science, history, information science, systems theory, communication theory, artificial intelligence, and psychology" (*Organization Science*, 2007). Table 3-8 represents project management research trends in *Organization Science*.

There were only five project management related papers (13 occurrences) in *Organization Science* since the journal started its first edition in the early 1990s. Because of the unique goals and characteristics of *Organization Science*, OB/HRM (38%) and STRATEGY/PPM (23%) were the two areas that had most occurrences. Two papers addressed new product development projects (Gerwin & Ferris, 2004; Li, Bingham, & Umphress, 2007), one paper looked at the Sydney Olympics (Pitsis & Clegg, 2003) and others looked at research oriented organizations (O'Connor, Rice, Peters, & Veryzer, 2003) and systems development teams (Kirsch, 1996). There were no occurrences in the areas of EC/CONTRACT/LEGAL, PERFORMANCE/EVM, or QM/6SIGMA/PI.

3.3.5 *Information Systems Research*

Information Systems Research is a "leading international journal of theory, research, and intellectual development, focused on information systems in organizations, institutions, the economy, and society. It is dedicated to furthering knowledge in the productive application of information technologies to human organizations and their management and, more broadly, to improved economic and social welfare" (*Information Systems Research*, 2007).

ISR was first published in the 1990s. There were 17 articles (32 occurrences) published in *Information Systems Research* and all 17 focused on IT/IS. Unlike other INFORMS journals, PERFORMANCE/

No.	Allied Disciplines	50–59	60–69	70–79	80–89	90–99	00–07	TOTAL	%
1	OR/DS/OM/SCM	X	X	X	X	1	1	2	15%
2	OB/HRM	X	X	X	X	1	4	5	38%
3	IT/IS	X	X	X	X	1	0	1	8%
4	TECH/INNOV/NPD/R&D	X	X	X	X	0	2	2	15%
5	EC/CONTRACT/LEGAL	X	X	X	X	0		0	0%
6	STRATEGY/PPM	X	X	X	X	0	3	3	23%
7	PERFORMANCE/EVM	X	X	X	X	0	0	0	0%
8	QM/6SIGMA/PI	X	X	X	X	0	0	0	0%
	TOTAL	X	X	X	X	3	10	13	100%
	PERCENTAGE	0%	0%	0%	0%	23%	77%	100%	

Table 3-8   Project Management Research Trends in
          Organization Science

EVM (16%) was the second most popular subject (Fichman, 2004; Ranganathan & Brown, 2006; Banker & Slaughter, 2000; Guinan, Cooprider, & Faraj, 1998; Jain, Tanniru, & Fazlollahi, 1991) after IT/IS (47%). OR/DS/OM/SCM (9%) was not a popular subject for this journal as compared to *Management Science* and *Operations Research* journals (see Table 3-9).

3.3.6 Project Management Research Trends in INFORMS Journals

To better analyze and understand the overall trends of project management research from the Institute for Operations Research and the Management Sciences (INFORMS), five journals have been combined and the results are shown in Table 3-10 and Figure 3-2.

STRATEGY/PPM (31%) and OR/DS/OM/SCM (30%) were the two major disciplines where project management research appeared most in INFORMS journals, followed by IT/IS (12%), PERFORM/EVM (8%) and TECH/INNOV/NPD/R&D (7%). Other disciplines such as OB/HRM (6%), EC/CONTRACT/LEGAL (4%), and QM/6SIGMA/PI (2%), did not have a major presence in project management research. There was a big jump in terms of project management research from the 1960s (6%) to the 1970s (20%), reached a plateau during the 1980s (19%), and then started to show renewal of interest in the 1990s (25%) and 2000s (29%).

3.4 Practitioner Journals

Project management as a practice comes from engineering-construction, defense, and lately the IT/IS sector beginning in the 1980s. It is important to note that there are many important key journals dedi-

No.	Allied Disciplines	50–59	60–69	70–79	80–89	90–99	00–07	TOTAL	%
1	OR/DS/OM/SCM	X	X	X	X	2	1	3	9%
2	OB/HRM	X	X	X	X	3	0	3	9%
3	IT/IS	X	X	X	X	7	10	17	47%
4	TECH/INNOV/NPD/R&D	X	X	X	X	1	2	3	9%
5	EC/CONTRACT/LEGAL	X	X	X	X	1	0	1	3%
6	STRATEGY/PPM	X	X	X	X	1	0	1	3%
7	PERFORMANCE/EVM	X	X	X	X	2	3	5	16%
8	QM/6SIGMA/PI	X	X	X	X	1	0	1	3%
	TOTAL	X	X	X	X	18	16	32	100%
	PERCENTAGE	0%	0%	0%	0%	56%	50%	100%	

Table 3-9   Project Management Research Trends in *Information Systems Research*

No.	Allied Disciplines	50–59	60–69	70–79	80–89	90–99	00–07	TOTAL	%
1	OR/DS/OM/SCM	2	10	29	23	24	26	114	30%
2	OB/HRM	0	2	4	2	9	7	24	6%
3	IT/IS	2	2	4	6	15	18	45	12%
4	TECH/INNOV/NPD/R&D	0	1	3	7	4	12	27	7%
5	EC/CONTRACT/LEGAL	1	1	2	2	5	4	15	4%
6	STRATEGY/PPM	1	4	23	30	27	31	116	31%
7	PERFORMANCE/EVM	1	2	8	3	6	10	30	8%
8	QM/6SIGMA/PI	0	1	2	0	3	1	7	2%
	TOTAL	7	23	75	73	93	109	378	100%
	PERCENTAGE	2%	6%	20%	19%	25%	29%	100%	0

Table 3-10   Project Management Research Trends in INFORMS Journals

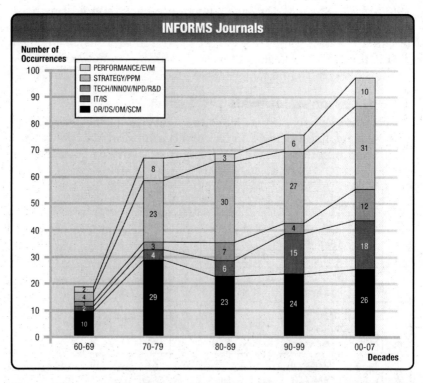

Figure 3-2   Project Management Research Trends in INFORMS Journals

cated to these specific areas. For the purpose of our study, we focused only on top management journals and excluded other respected journals in their relevant fields.

As we discussed in Chapter 2, we believe that project management evolved from three major roots from the management school's perspectives: (1) organizational management theory (AOM); (2) operations research and management science applications (INFORMS); and (3) real business practices and their applications. *Academy of Management Perspectives* and *Interfaces* were categorized into the appropriate academic/professional societies. This was done to analyze the trends of their societies even though the goals and objectives of these journals are business and practice-oriented.

We have identified and selected four journals that are practice-oriented: *Harvard Business Review, California Management Review, Sloan Management Review,* and *Long Range Planning.* The following sections analyze in detail the project management research and publication trends of these journals.

3.4.1 *Harvard Business Review*

Harvard Business Review is a general management magazine published since 1922 by Harvard Business School Publishing, owned by the Harvard Business School. A monthly research-based magazine written for business practitioners, it claims a high ranking in business readership and enjoys the reverence of academics, executives, and management consultants. "The Harvard Business Review has one goal: to be the source of the best new ideas for people creating, leading, and transforming business. HBR's articles cover a wide range of topics that are relevant to different industries, management functions, and geographic locations. They focus on such areas as leadership, organizational change, negotiation, strategy, operations, marketing, finance, and managing people. They are written for senior managers by experts whose authority comes from careful analysis, study, and experience. The ideas presented in these articles can be translated into action and have been tested in the real world of business" (Harvard Business Review, 2007).

Table 3-11 shows the analysis of project management research trends in the *Harvard Business Review.* STRATEGY/PPM (30%) had the most occurrences in its articles, which aligns well with the publication's objectives, followed by OR/DS/OM/SCM (20%), OB/HRM (19%), and PERFORMANCE/EVM (16%) (Mankins & Steele, 2005) (Fleming & Koppelman, 2003) (Engwall & Svensson, 2001). The trend of publishing project management research in HBR went down in the 1970s (14%) and the 1990s (16%) and up during the 1960s (19%), 1980s (25%), and 2000s (22%). It seems that publication

No.	Allied Disciplines	50–59	60–69	70–79	80–89	90–99	00–07	TOTAL	%
1	OR/DS/OM/SCM	1	3	2	3	2	2	13	20%
2	OB/HRM	1	0	3	3	2	3	12	19%
3	IT/IS	0	0	1	1	0	0	2	3%
4	TECH/INNOV/NPD/R&D	0	2	0	0	0	0	2	3%
5	EC/CONTRACT/LEGAL	0	1	1	2	0	0	4	6%
6	STRATEGY/PPM	1	2	1	6	4	5	19	30%
7	PERFORMANCE/EVM	0	4	1	0	1	4	10	16%
8	QM/6SIGMA/PI	0	0	0	1	1	0	2	3%
	TOTAL	3	12	9	16	10	14	64	100%
	PERCENTAGE	5%	19%	14%	25%	16%	22%	100%	

Table 3-11   Project Management Research Trends in *Harvard Business Review*

of project management research has gone up and down over the last 40 years in HBR. One explanation might be that during the 1960s (19%) and 1980s (25%) project management practitioners had more interest in project management while during the 1970s (14%) and 1990s (16%), academic scholars seemed to have more interest in project management.

3.4.2 *California Management Review*

California Management Review interprets management broadly "to include subject matter taught in business schools as well as work in other fields that is applicable to management functions and practices. CMR typically publishes articles that extend our knowledge of a given topic either by building upon existing theories or by presenting new empirical work. CMR is particularly interested in manuscripts that focus on corporate strategy and organization, the management of technology, business and public policy, and managing in the global business economy" (*California Management Review*, 2007).

CMR started to show strong interest in project management in the 1990s (22%) and beyond. More that 60% of the occurrences in its papers were published during the 1990s (22%) and 2000s (42%). OB/HRM (20%), IT/IS (18%), and TECH/INNOV/NPD/R&D (16%) were the three areas that were addressed in more than 50% of its occurrences of project management research. QM/6SIGMA/PI (2%) was the least addressed subject (Price & Chan, 1993). CMR is planning to publish a special issue on "Infrastructure Privatization: Frameworks and Tools for a Regulated Setting," which shows a continuing interest in project management research and applications. CMR also published several articles related to high-technology management, information systems technology, and practices in the Silicon Valley area, a specific trait of this journal. Table 3-12 represents project management research trends in *California Management Review*.

3.4.3 *Sloan Management Review*

Massachusetts Institute of Technology's *Sloan Management Review* is a "peer-reviewed academic journal covering all management disciplines, although its particular emphasis is on corporate strategy, leadership and management of technology and innovation. It bridges the gap between management research and practice, evaluating and reporting on new research to help readers identify and understand significant trends in management. SMR is known internationally as a trusted source of useful and innovative ideas for business leaders" (*Sloan Management Review*, 2007).

Similar to *Harvard Business Review*, STRATEGY/PPM (38%), and OB/HRM (27%) were the two areas that had the most occurrences of project management research in papers in SMR followed by OR/DS/OM/SCM (12%) and TECH/INNOV/NPD/R&D (12%). There were no occurrences in the areas of EC/CONTRACT/LEGAL or QM/6SIGMA/PI. Also, it is interesting to note that there is a strong upward trend in publication of project management research in SMR beginning in the 1970s (27%), and that continued into the 1980s (38%) and 1990s (35%). Table 3-13 represents the subjects that SMR published over the past decades. (Please note that we were only able to search the database up to 1997, so the analysis might not be current for SMR.)

No.	Allied Disciplines	50–59	60–69	70–79	80–89	90–99	00–07	TOTAL	%
1	OR/DS/OM/SCM	X	2	1	0	3	0	6	12%
2	OB/HRM	X	1	2	0	1	6	10	20%
3	IT/IS	X	0	1	0	1	7	9	18%
4	TECH/INNOV/NPD/R&D	X	2	0	1	3	2	8	16%
5	EC/CONTRACT/LEGAL	X	3	0	0	1	0	4	8%
6	STRATEGY/PPM	X	1	1	2	1	1	6	12%
7	PERFORMANCE/EVM	X	0	0	1	0	5	6	12%
8	QM/6SIGMA/PI	X	0	0	0	1	0	1	2%
	TOTAL	X	9	5	4	11	21	50	100%
	PERCENTAGE	0%	18%	10%	8%	22%	42%	100%	

Table 3-12   Project Management Research Trends in *California Management Review*

No.	Allied Disciplines	50–59	60–69	70–79	80–89	90–99	00–07	TOTAL	%
1	OR/DS/OM/SCM	X	0	X	2	1	X	3	12%
2	OB/HRM	X	0	3	2	2	X	7	27%
3	IT/IS	X	0	0	1	1	X	2	8%
4	TECH/INNOV/NPD/R&D	X	0	0	2	1	X	3	12%
5	EC/CONTRACT/LEGAL	X	0	0	0	0	X	0	0%
6	STRATEGY/PPM	X	0	4	3	3	X	10	38%
7	PERFORMANCE/EVM	X	0	0	0	1	X	1	4%
8	QM/6SIGMA/PI	X	0	0	0	0	X	0	0%
	TOTAL	X	0	7	10	9	X	26	100%
	PERCENTAGE	0%	0%	27%	38%	35%	X%	100%	

Table 3-13   Project Management Research Trends in *Sloan Management Review*

3.4.4 *Long Range Planning*

Long Range Planning is one of the leading international journals in the field of strategic management, and it is published six times a year. "It features articles which offer original research that bridge the gap between academia and practice. The goal of LRP is influence the behavior of senior managers, administrators and to influence academic thinking. It is an essential reading for senior managers, and those involved in executive education" (*Long Range Planning*, 2007).

Long Range Planning had 56 papers (83 occurrences) during the last 40 years (see Table 3-14). There were many papers related to project management particularly during the 1980s (31%) and 1990s

No.	Allied Disciplines	50–59	60–69	70–79	80–89	90–99	00–07	TOTAL	%
1	OR/DS/OM/SCM	X	X	0	7	1	0	8	10%
2	OB/HRM	X	X	1	0	1	1	3	4%
3	IT/IS	X	X	0	2	2	0	4	5%
4	TECH/INNOV/NPD/R&D	X	X	4	1	7	5	17	20%
5	EC/CONTRACT/LEGAL	X	X	0	0	2	1	3	4%
6	STRATEGY/PPM	X	X	9	16	13	6	44	53%
7	PERFORMANCE/EVM	X	X	1	0	2	1	4	5%
8	QM/6SIGMA/PI	X	X	0	0	0	0	0	0%
	TOTAL	X	X	15	26	28	14	83	100%
	PERCENTAGE	0%	0%	18%	31%	34%	17%	100%	

Table 3-14   Project Management Research Trends in *Long Range Planning*

(34%). Since the new editorial direction of the journal in the early 2000s, far fewer papers on project management appeared in recent years. Because of the "strategic nature" of the journal, STRATEGY/ PPM accounts for over 50% of the occurrences followed by TECH/ INNOV/NPD/R&D (20%) and OR/DS/OM/SCM (10%). There were no papers from the QM/6SIGMA/PI area.

3.4.5 Project Management Research Trends in Combined Practitioner Journals

To analyze and better understand the overall trends of project management research from the practitioner journals perspective, *Harvard Business Review, California Management Review, Sloan Management Review*, and *Long Range Planning* were combined. Table 3-15 presents the analysis of practitioner journals, and Figure 3-3 shows the overall project management research trends in the combined journals.

Based on trend analyses, STRATEGY/PPM (35%), OB/HRM (14%), OR/DS/OM/SCM (13%), and TECH/INNOV/NPD/R&D (13%) were the four disciplines that dealt most with topics related to project management. PERFORMANCE/EVM (9%), IT/IS (8%), and OB/HRM (14%) are the areas that have been gaining more interest over the past decades, and STRATEGY/PPM (35%) and OR/DS/OM/ SCM (14%) are the areas that have been declining in terms of research interests. We thought that QM/6SIGMA/PI (1%) would be more widely published because of its practice-oriented, strategic subject; however, it did not really show strong interest in practitioner journals. It seems that QM/6SIGMA/PI still has not received the proper recognition and popularity that it deserves among practitioner journals.

No.	Allied Disciplines	50–59	60–69	70–79	80–89	90–99	00–07	TOTAL	%
1	OR/DS/OM/SCM	1	5	3	12	7	2	30	13%
2	OB/HRM	1	1	9	5	6	10	32	14%
3	IT/IS	0	0	2	4	4	7	17	8%
4	TECH/INNOV/NPD/R&D	0	4	4	4	11	7	30	13%
5	EC/CONTRACT/LEGAL	0	4	1	2	3	1	11	5%
6	STRATEGY/PPM	1	3	15	27	21	12	79	35%
7	PERFORMANCE/EVM	0	4	2	1	4	10	21	9%
8	QM/6SIGMA/PI	0	0	0	1	2	0	3	1%
	TOTAL	3	21	36	56	58	49	223	100%
	PERCENTAGE	1%	9%	16%	25%	26%	22%	100%	0

Table 3-15   Project Management Research Trends in Practitioner Journals

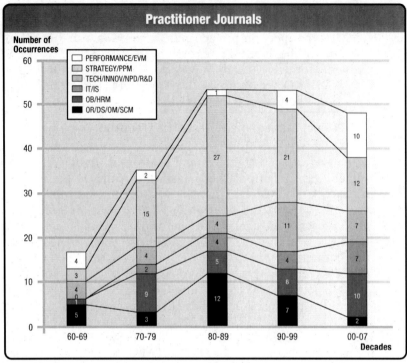

Figure 3-3   Project Management Research Trends in Practitioner Journals

3.5 *IEEE Transactions of Engineering Management* (From 1988)

IEEE Transactions of Engineering Management is one of the most prestigious journals in the engineering management field and has been published since 1954. It publishes papers in the area of "the management sciences and technology applicable to individuals and organizations engaged in or overseeing the management of engineering or technology including: technology policy development, technology assessment, technology transfer, research, development, design, evaluation, production, commissioning, or decommissioning of technical, electrical or electronic equipment/systems and allied activities" (IEEE TEM, 2007).

Since *IEEE Explore* allows users to search papers for the last 20 years only, we were only able to analyze project management trends starting from 1988. STRATEGY/PPM (25%) and TECH/INNOV/NPD/R&D (23%) were the two major areas that made up half of the research subject occurrences. EC/CONTRACT/LEGAL (2%) and QM/6SIGMA/PI (2%) are the two areas that had the least appearance in IEEE TEM. From the 1990s (41%) and into the 2000s (56%), there has been increasing occurrences of publication of research in the areas of IT/IS (15%) and TECH/INNOV/NPD/R&D (23%). In contrast, STRATEGY/PPM (25%), OB/HRM (13%), and OR/DS/OM/SCM (16%) have reached a plateau with no substantial changes in the number of occurrences of publications. Overall, there is a steady increase in project management related occurrences of publications. Table 3-16 and Figure 3-4 represent the publication trends of project management research from 1988.

3.6 Other Journals

3.6.1 *Journal of Operations Management*

The mission of the *Journal of Operations Management* is to publish original, high-quality research papers in the field of operations management. "The topic covered in JOM includes: Operations management in process, manufacturing, and service organizations; Operations strategy and policy; Product and service design and development; Manufacturing and service systems design; Technology management for operations; Multi-site operations management; Capacity planning and analysis; Operations planning, scheduling and control; Project management; Human resource management for operations; Work design, measurement, and improvement; Performance measurement and productivity; Quality management; Purchasing/sourcing systems; Materials and inventory management; Logistics, transportation, distribution, and materials handling; International and comparative operations; Operations information man-

No.	Allied Disciplines	50–59	60–69	70–79	80–89	90–99	00–07	TOTAL	%
1	OR/DS/OM/SCM	X	X	X	0	15	15	27	16%
2	OB/HRM	X	X	X	0	11	13	22	13%
3	IT/IS	X	X	X	1	8	18	21	15%
4	TECH/INNOV/NPD/R&D	X	X	X	0	18	25	34	23%
5	EC/CONTRACT/LEGAL	X	X	X	0	1	3	3	2%
6	STRATEGY/PPM	X	X	X	3	21	23	47	25%
7	PERFORMANCE/EVM	X	X	X	1	2	3	6	3%
8	QM/6SIGMA/PI	X	X	X	0	0	4	3	2%
	TOTAL	X	X	X	5	76	104	185	100%
	PERCENTAGE	0%	0%	0%	3%	41%	56%	100%	

Table 3-16   Project Management Research Trends in *IEEE Transactions on Engineering Management*

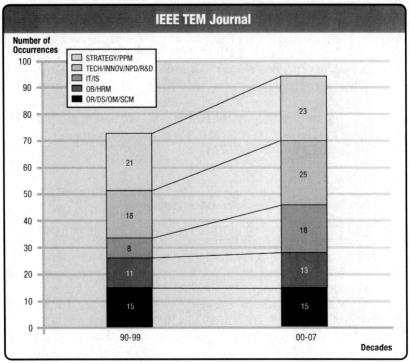

Figure 3-4   Project Management Research Trends in *IEEE Transactions of Engineering Management*

agement; Regulatory and environmental issues in operations" (*Journal of Operations Management*, 2007).

Table 3-17 shows that OR/DS/OM/SVM (43%) and STRATEGY/PPM (25%) were the two areas that had most occurrences followed by TECH/INNOV/NPD/R&D (12%) and PERFORMANCE/EVM (10%). The other disciplines had very few occurrences in papers in their respected areas. Occurrences of publications show overall increasing trends. More detailed analysis reveals that OR/DS/OM/SCM decreased by about 50% and STRATEGY/PPM increased by about 75% between the 1990s and the 2000s.

3.6.2 *MIS Quarterly*

The objective of *MIS Quarterly* (MISQ) is "the enhancement and communication of knowledge concerning the development of IT-based services, the management of information technology resources, and the economics and use of information technology with managerial and organizational implications" (*MIS Quarterly*, 2007).

No.	Allied Disciplines	50–59	60–69	70–79	80–89	90–99	00–07	TOTAL	%
1	OR/DS/OM/SCM	X	X	X	6	11	5	22	43%
2	OB/HRM	X	X	X	0	0	1	1	2%
3	IT/IS	X	X	X	1	1	0	2	4%
4	TECH/INNOV/NPD/R&D	X	X	X	0	3	3	6	12%
5	EC/CONTRACT/LEGAL	X	X	X	0	0	0	0	0%
6	STRATEGY/PPM	X	X	X	2	4	7	13	25%
7	PERFORMANCE/EVM	X	X	X	3	0	2	5	10%
8	QM/6SIGMA/PI	X	X	X	0	0	1	1	2%
	TOTAL	X	X	X	12	19	19	50	100%
	PERCENTAGE	0%	0%	0%	24%	38%	38%	100%	

Table 3-17   Project Management Research Trends in *Journal of Operations Management*

Table 3-18 shows that IT/IS (46%), STRATEGY/PPM (22%), and OB/HRM (12%) were the three areas that had the most occurrences in paper publications in MISQ. Perhaps IT/IS (46%) appeared because of the nature of this journal, STRATEGY/PPM (22%) appeared because of the managerial and strategic implications, and OB/HRM (12%) appeared because of a strong interest in organizational implications. Occurrences in paper publications reached its peak in the 1980s (68%), then declined sharply in the 1990s and 2000s. This is an interesting trend, but probably only applies to *MIS Quarterly*. In fact, there are many papers published on IT project management in other IT/IS related journals, but we believe that because of the edito-

No.	Allied Disciplines	50–59	60–69	70–79	80–89	90–99	00–07	TOTAL	%
1	OR/DS/OM/SCM	X	X	0	2	0	0	2	5%
2	OB/HRM	X	X	0	3	2	0	5	12%
3	IT/IS	X	X	1	12	5	1	19	46%
4	TECH/INNOV/NPD/R&D	X	X	0	1	0	1	2	5%
5	EC/CONTRACT/LEGAL	X	X	0	0	0	0	0	0%
6	STRATEGY/PPM	X	X	0	7	2	0	9	22%
7	PERFORMANCE/EVM	X	X	0	2	0	0	2	5%
8	QM/6SIGMA/PI	X	X	1	1	0	0	2	5%
	TOTAL	X	X	2	28	9	2	41	100%
	PERCENTAGE	0%	0%	5%	68%	22%	5%	100%	

Table 3-18   Project Management Research Trends in *MIS Quarterly*

rial direction of *MIS Quarterly*, there were not many papers dealing with project management research.

3.6.3 *Strategic Management Journal*

Strategic Management Journal publishes original material concerned with all aspects of strategic management. "It is devoted to the improvement and further development of the theory and practice of strategic management and it is designed to appeal to both practicing managers and academics. Overall, SMJ provides a communication forum for advancing strategic management theory and practice. Such major topics as strategic resource allocation; organization structure; leadership; entrepreneurship and organizational purpose; methods and techniques for evaluating and understanding competitive, technological, social, and political environments; planning processes; and strategic decision processes are included" (*Strategic Management Journal*, 2007).

STRATEGY/PPM (57%) and TECH/INNOV/NPD/R&D (14%) had over 70% of the occurrences and were the two major topics that integrated project management applications with their research interests. There were no occurrences in the areas of EC/CONTRACT/LEGAL and QM/6SIGMA/PI. Occurrences have decreased from the 1990s to the 2000s. It seems that interest in publishing project management related papers has not increased over the last 20 years, indicating that SMJ might not be a proper venue to publish papers related to project management. Table 3-19 presents project management research trends in *Strategic Management Journal*.

No.	Allied Disciplines	50–59	60–69	70–79	80–89	90–99	00–07	TOTAL	%
1	OR/DS/OM/SCM	X	X	X	0	1	0	1	7%
2	OB/HRM	X	X	X	0	1	0	1	7%
3	IT/IS	X	X	X	0	1	0	1	7%
4	TECH/INNOV/NPD/R&D	X	X	X	0	2	0	2	14%
5	EC/CONTRACT/LEGAL	X	X	X	0	0	0	0	0%
6	STRATEGY/PPM	X	X	X	1	3	4	8	57%
7	PERFORMANCE/EVM	X	X	X	0	0	1	1	7%
8	QM/6SIGMA/PI	X	X	X	0	0	0	0	0%
	TOTAL	X	X	X	1	8	5	14	100%
	PERCENTAGE	0%	0%	0%	7%	57%	36%	100%	

Table 3-19   Project Management Research Trends in *Strategic Management Journal*

3.6.4 *Administrative Science Quarterly*

Administrative Science Quarterly publishes "the best organizational theory papers from a number of disciplines, including organizational behavior and theory, sociology, psychology and social psychology, strategic management, economics, public administration, and industrial relations" (*Administrative Science Quarterly* 2007). Table 3-20 presents the trends of ASQ research related to project management. There were a total of three papers related to project management published in the 1960s, 1970s, and 1980s (Burack, 1967; Carter, 1971; Burns, 1989). An explanation could be that *Administrative Science Quarterly* is not an appropriate outlet for publishing papers in project management.

3.6.5 *Journal of Small Business Management*

Journal of Small Business Management publishes "scholarly research articles in the fields of small business management and entrepreneurship. As the official journal of the International Council for Small Business (ICSB), the JSBM is recognized as a primary instrument for projecting and supporting the goals and objectives of this organization, which include scholarly research and the free exchange of ideas. The journal, which is circulated in 60 countries around the world, is a leader in the field of small business research" (*Journal of Small Business Management*, 2007). There was only one paper published in the *JSBM* that discussed the applications of project management by small business to develop new products and services (Larson & Gobeli, 1991).

No.	Allied Disciplines	50–59	60–69	70–79	80–89	90–99	00–07	TOTAL	%
1	OR/DS/OM/SCM	X	1	1	0	0	0	2	33%
2	OB/HRM	X	1	1	1	0	0	3	50%
3	IT/IS	X	0	0	0	0	0	0	0%
4	TECH/INNOV/NPD/R&D	X	0	0	0	0	0	0	0%
5	EC/CONTRACT/LEGAL	X	0	0	0	0	0	0	0%
6	STRATEGY/PPM	X	0	0	1	0	0	1	17%
7	PERFORMANCE/EVM	X	0	0	0	0	0	0	0%
8	QM/6SIGMA/PI	X	0	0	0	0	0	0	0%
	TOTAL	X	2	2	2	0	0	6	100%
	PERCENTAGE	0%	33%	33%	33%	0%	0%	100%	

Table 3-20   Project Management Research Trends in *Administrative Science Quarterly*

3.7 Discussions and Conclusions

Table 3-21 and Figure 3-5 provide an analysis of research trends of project management in allied disciplines from top management journals. Ranking of occurrences of the eight disciplines from most to the least appeared subjects over the last 50 years is:

1. STRATEGY/PPM (30%)
2. OR/DS/OM/SCM (23%)
3. OB/HRM (13%)
4. IT/IS (11%)
5. TECH/INNOV/NPD/R&D (11%)
6. PERFORMANCE/EVM (7%)
7. EC/CONTRACT/LEGAL (3%)
8. QM/6SIGMA/PI (2%)

Based on this analysis, STRATEGY/PPM and OR/DS/OM/SCM represent more than 50% of the occurrences in publication of project management related research. However, STRATEGY/PPM, TECH/INNOV/NPD/R&D, IT/IS, and PERFORMANCE/EVM are the four disciplines that show large increases in occurrences in publications and are expected to continue to have strong upward trends in publication of project management related research in the foreseeable future. These four areas represent the disciplines in which scholars' research interests are currently focused and appear to have great research potential in the future.

In contrast, occurrences in publication of project management related research in the area of OR/DS/OM/SCM and OB/HRM peaked during the 1990s, but the occurrences have slowed down in

Allied Disciplines	50–59	60–69	70–79	80–89	90–99	00–07	TOTAL	%
OR/DS/OM/SCM	3	20	37	49	65	54	228	23%
OB/HRM	1	5	18	14	46	43	127	13%
IT/IS	2	2	7	22	35	37	105	11%
TECH/INNOV/NPD/R&D	0	1	12	13	39	46	111	11%
EC/CONTRACT/LEGAL	1	4	2	4	10	7	28	3%
STRATEGY/PPM	2	10	48	74	78	83	295	30%
PERFORMANCE/EVM	1	6	10	11	12	28	68	7%
QM/6SIGMA/PI	0	1	2	1	7	7	18	2%
TOTAL	10	49	136	188	292	305	980	100%
PERCENTAGE	1%	5%	14%	19%	30%	31%	100%	

Table 3-21   Research Trends of Project Management Allied Disciplines

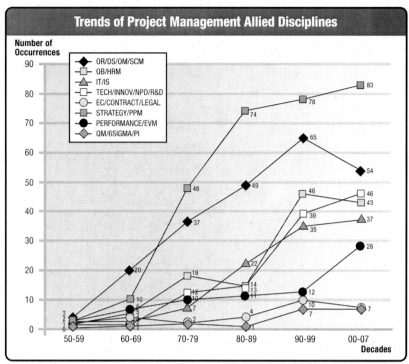

Figure 3-5   Research Trends of Project Management Allied Disciplines (1950s to 2007)

the 2000s. These two disciplines are two of the three origins of project management, and it seems that research output in these areas has matured with a possible continuing downward trend for OR/DS/OM/SCM in the future.

EC/CONTRACT/LEGAL and QM/6SIGMA/PI did not really gain any momentum in occurrences of research output from the management research community. It is important to note that these two areas are having great success in publication in relevant journals in their fields but appear to struggle when it comes to publication in the top management journals. Because of the practical nature of these two disciplines, it seems that the management scholars' community is strongly resisting acceptance of these two areas as mainstream management research.

Table 3-22 and Figure 3-6 represent occurrences of project management research in the allied disciplines analyzed by decade using the 18 top management and business journal publications.

QM/6SIGMA/PI, EC/CONTRACT/LEGAL, and PERFORMANCE/EVM were not able to penetrate mainstream management research.

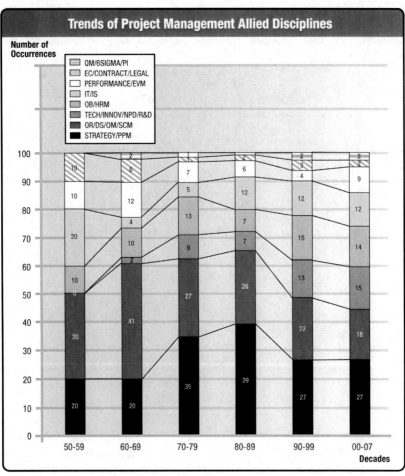

Figure 3-6   Research Trends of Project Management Allied
Disciplines by Decade

Research in IT/IS was active in the 1980s, reached its peak, and then flattened out. Research in OB/HRM was strong up to the 1970s then slowed down during the 1980s when project management research focused more on processes, tools, and techniques, then regained interest in the 1990s and flattened out. TECH/INNOV/NPD/R&D is probably the only area that showed an upward trend since the 1960s. The research proportion of OR/DS/OM/SCM peaked during the 1960s, and from the 1970s the relative proportion has been getting smaller and smaller. STRATEGY/PPM was most popular in the 1980s and became flat in the 1990s. It is important to note that in the 2000s, STRATEGY/PPM was the most popular subject. However, research in other disciplines has increased proportionally more rapidly.

Allied Disciplines	50–59	60–69	70–79	80–89	90–99	00–07	TOTAL
STRATEGY/PPM	20%	20%	35%	39%	27%	27%	295
OR/DS/OM/SCM	30%	41%	27%	26%	22%	18%	228
TECH/INNOV/NPD/R&D	0%	2%	9%	7%	13%	15%	111
OB/HRM	10%	10%	13%	7%	16%	14%	127
IT/IS	20%	4%	5%	12%	12%	12%	105
PERFORMANCE/EVM	10%	12%	7%	6%	4%	9%	68
EC/CONTRACT/LEGAL	10%	8%	1%	2%	3%	2%	28
QM/6SIGMA/PI	0%	2%	1%	1%	2%	2%	18
TOTAL	100%	100%	100%	100%	100%	100%	980

Table 3-22   Research Trends of Project Management Allied Disciplines by Decade

To summarize, STRATEGY/PPM is still a very important project management research subject among the eight disciplines in the 18 top management and business journals. It seems that the strong trend of STRATEGY/PPM (27%) will continue in the future. It is interesting to note that OR/DS/OM/SCM (18%), TECH/INNOV/NPD/R&D (15%), OB/HRM (14%), IT/IS (12%), and even PERFORMANCE/EVM (9%) are all starting to have substantial shares in project management research, which is a very positive sign for project management scholars. QM/6SIGMA/PI and EC/CONTRACT/LEGAL are the two disciplines struggling to position themselves in the top management and business journals, and it is likely that this trend will continue in the future.

CHAPTER 4

The Future of Project Management and Allied Disciplines

4.1 Introduction

A survey using the World Wide Web was conducted to explore the impact on project management trends in the allied disciplines. The purpose of the survey was to collect academicians' and practitioners' perceptions on the trends, impact, and challenges relevant to project management. We asked the respondents to reflect on their best understanding of the availability and impact of research in the allied disciplines on project management applications by decade starting from the 1960s to the 2000s and into future. We also asked several important open-ended questions to collect and analyze respondents' views on trends in the allied disciplines and their impact on project management in the past as well as their predictions on the future of project management. All responses were kept anonymous to obtain unbiased and honest responses.

We announced the study through key project management list servs, posted the survey to the PMI research survey Web site, and asked students and alumni of The George Washington University's Master of Science in Project Management program to participate in the survey. Overall, we received 82 responses over a period of five months. We were relatively disappointed with the low response rate to this very important survey.

However, when we looked at the survey participants, we observed that they are focused groups who are all part of the project management community either as a practitioners, consultants, scholars, or other professionals working in the project management environment. We were able to collect rich, qualitative information and opinions from the participants by asking open-ended questions regarding trends and the future of project management and its allied disciplines.

We also conducted face-to-face and telephone, in-depth interviews to collect thoughts from project management scholars and practitioners concerning trends in the allied disciplines and their potential impact on the future of project management.

The thoughts collected in the survey of the project management community and the interviews provided valuable insights in identifying trends in the allied disciplines and their impact on the future of project management, as well as the opportunities, challenges, and obstacles that are likely to persist or materialize in the future.

4.2 Survey Respondents' Demographics

A total of 82 responses were collected from the Web-based survey. Approximately 98% of the respondents had earned a bachelor's degree or higher: 32% were bachelor's degree holders: 50% were master's degree holders, and 16% were doctoral degree holders. Table 4-1 shows the distribution in detail.

Next, we asked respondents their years of work experiences. Almost 90% worked for more than five years in the project management field, and among them about 46% worked for more than 20 years. Table 4-2 summarizes respondents' years of experiences.

The respondents' occupations were diverse yet focused on the project management field: 12% were academic scholars, 11% were graduate students, 44% were project management practitioners, and 16% were consultants/trainers. Others included federal government capital planning specialists, engineers, program analyst, and project directors. Table 4-3 summarizes the distribution of respondents' occupations.

Education	Response Percentage	Response Count
High school degree	1.2%	1
Two-year associate degree	1.2%	1
Four-year bachelor degree	31.7%	26
Master's degree	*50%*	*41*
Doctoral degree	15.9%	13
Total	**100%**	**82**

Table 4-1   Respondents' Education

Years of Work Experience	Response Percentage	Response Count
Less than 2 years	4.9%	4
2 to 5 years	7.3%	6
6 to 10 years	11.0%	9
11 to 15 years	15.9%	13
16 to 20 years	14.6%	12
More than 20 years	*46.3%*	*38*
Total	**100%**	**82**

Table 4-2   Respondents' Years of Work Experiences

Occupation	Response Percentage	Response Count
Academicians (professor or researcher)	12.2%	10
Student	11.0%	9
Project management practitioner	*43.9%*	*36*
Consultant/trainer	15.9%	13
Other (please specify)	17.1%	14
Total	**100%**	**82**

Table 4-3   Respondents' Occupations

To summarize, project management practitioners with a master's degree who have 20 years or more experience are the ones that best represent the respondents.

4.3 Survey Results and Analysis

In the questions numbered from 1 to 16, we asked respondents to reflect their best understanding of the availability and impact on project management of research and applications in other disciplines by decade. The results showed generally that there is a growing upward trend in terms of both availability and impact of research and applications in the allied disciplines related to project management. Detailed response results to questions 1 through 16 are shown in Appendix B.

From questions numbered 17 to 21, we asked open-ended questions where respondents could express their thoughts and opinions. Respondents were asked to assess the past, present and future of project management practice and discipline. We summarized the respondents' opinions in a narrative form to capture past trends, current status, and future of project management from the perspective of core project management community.

We specifically asked about the availability of knowledge (articles, literature, and experts) and the potential impact of allied disciplines related to project management. We were able to assess where the allied disciplines currently stand in terms of availability and impact as well as make meaningful predictions about the future. We used a 1 to 7 Likert scale to capture the respondents' assessment. Then we used a 2×2 matrix to understand where each allied discipline currently stands relative to other disciplines. We summarized the results so that each quadrant has low or high availability and impact. Figure 4-1 shows the four quadrants we used to portray the results. Based on the responses, we plotted the eight disciplines relative to each other using this availability-impact scheme. Figures 4-2 and 4-3 show the current trends of allied disciplines as they relate to project management.

OB/HRM, TECH/INNOV/NPD/R&D, STRATEGY/PPM, and OR/DS/OM/SCM were the four disciplines that respondents perceived as low on availability of related knowledge and low on impact related to project management. It could be interpreted that these four disciplines still have potential for more research (availability) and could have potential for greater influence (impact) in the future. There was no discipline in the low availability-high impact quadrant. PERFORM/EVM and EC/CONTRACT/LEGAL were the two areas that respondents perceived as high in availability of related knowledge but low on impact related to project management. It could be interpreted that there is plenty of related information available currently; however, the impact on project management is low. QM/6SIGMA/PI and IT/IS were the two areas that were in the high

| Low Availability High Impact | High Availability High Impact |
| Low Availability Low Impact | High Availability Low Impact |

Figure 4-1   Availability-Impact Matrix

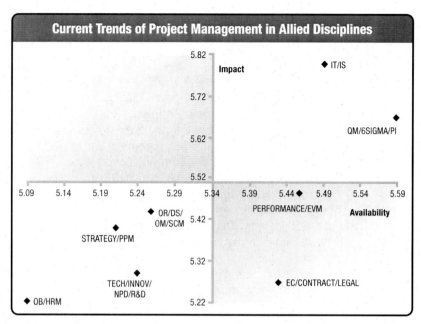

Figure 4-2   Current Trends of Project Management in Allied
              Disciplines

Low Availability, High Impact	High Availability, High Impact
None	QM/6SIGMA/PI
	IT/IS
Low Availability, Low Impact	High Availability, Low Impact
OB/HRM	PERFORMANCE/EVM
TECH/INNOV/NPD/R&D	EC/CONTRACT/LEGAL
STRATEGY/PPM	
OR/DS/OM/SCM	

Figure 4-3   Current Trends of Availability-Impact Matrix

availability and high impact quadrant. It could be interpreted that these two areas are the hot fields in project management currently.

We found some very interesting differences between the perceptions of the project management community and the actual research publications trends of allied disciplines by analyzing the 18 top management journals (see Table 3-21). As shown in Table 4-4, ranking of occurrences/availability of the two sets of data contradict each other substantially. We do not believe that there is anything wrong with the results or data. Analysis of the results clearly shows that research interests and publications in the top 18 management and business journals and the availability of actual knowledge and information from the project management community's perspective are different. The project management community relies on various sources of information besides top management journal articles including experts, trade magazines, conference presentations and proceedings, project management-focused journals, and newspapers to assess the trends of allied disciplines related to project management. Research trends in the top 18 management and business journals vs. the current impact on project management as viewed by the project management community also had no direct relationship between them (see Table 4-5).

We plotted the impact on project management of the eight allied disciplines from the perspective of the project management community vs. the total number of occurrences in publications in the top 18 management and business journals (see Figure 4-4).

By carefully considering Figure 4-4, we observe that (1) QM/6SIGMA/PI and IT/IS appear in the low availability, high-impact quadrant, which may highlight areas for relevant research and publications in the top 18 management and business journals in the areas of interest to the project management community; (2) STRATEGY/

Rankings	Research trends of allied disciplines related to project management from 18 top management journals from 2000–2007	Responses of project management community as to CURRENT availability of knowledge in allied disciplines related to project management
1	STRATEGY/PPM	QM/6SIGMA/PI
2	OR/DS/OM/SCM	IT/IS
3	TECH/INNOV/NPD/R&D	PERFORMANCE/EVM
4	OB/HRM	EC/CONTRACT/LEGAL
5	IT/IS	OR/DS/OM/SCM
6	PERFORMANCE/EVM	TECH/INNOV/NPD/R&D
7	EC/CONTRACT/LEGAL	STRATEGY/PPM
8	QM/6SIGMA/PI	OB/HRM

Table 4-4   Comparing Research Trends vs. Availability of Knowledge

Rankings	Research trends of allied disciplines related to project management from 18 top management journals from 2000–2007	Responses from project management community as to current impact of allied disciplines related to project management
1	STRATEGY/PPM	IT/IS
2	OR/DS/OM/SCM	QM/6SIGMA/PI
3	TECH/INNOV/NPD/R&D	PERFORMANCE/EVM
4	OB/HRM	OR/DS/OM/SCM
5	IT/IS	STRATEGY/PPM
6	PERFORMANCE/EVM	TECH/INNOV/NPD/R&D
7	EC/CONTRACT/LEGAL	EC/CONTRACT/LEGAL
8	QM/6SIGMA/PI	OB/HRM

Table 4-5   Comparing Research Trends vs. Impact on Project Management

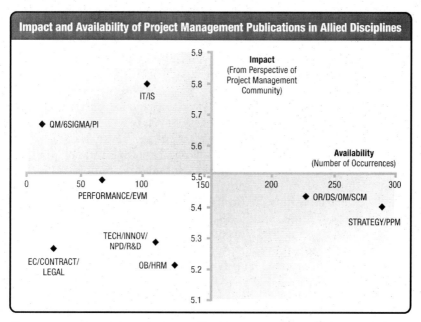

Figure 4-4   Current Impact (from perspective of the project management community) and Availability (in terms of number of total occurrences) of Project Management Publications in Allied Disciplines

PPM and OR/DS/OM/SCM appear in the high availability low impact quadrant, which may indicate that further research and publications in these areas have limited relevance to the project management community; (3) OB/HRM, TECH/INNOV/NPD/R&D, PERFORM/EVM, and EC/CONTRACT/LEGAL appear in the low availability, low impact quadrant, which may indicate that further research and publications in these areas could enhance the awareness and ensuing usage by the project management community of knowledge developed in these areas; and (4) none of the allied disciplines appears in the high availability, high impact quadrant, which may highlight areas for relevant research and publications in areas of high current interest to the project management community.

These interesting observations may provide valuable insights into the viewpoint of the project management community of the relevance of current publications of project management related research in the top 18 management and business journals. These observations may also highlight for management academic researchers and editors of the top 18 management and business journals areas in which further knowledge needs to be developed and disseminated to support the dynamic and growing discipline of project management and which will be viewed to be of particular relevance in the project management community.

We then plotted the eight allied disciplines relative to each other for the future trends of allied disciplines in project management. Figures 4-5 and 4-6 show the future trends of allied disciplines related to project management. OB/HRM, TECH/INNOV/NPD/R&D, and EC/CONTRACT/LEGAL were the three disciplines that respondents predict to be low on availability of related knowledge and low on impact related to project management in the future. There was no discipline that was in the low availability, high impact quadrant. OR/DS/OM/SCM was the area that respondents predicted to be high in availability of related knowledge but low on impact related to project management in the future. PERFORMANCE, QM/6SIGMA/PI, STRATEGY/PPM, and IT/IS were the four areas that were in the high availability and high-impact quadrant.

To better understand the project management community's perceptions of future trends of allied disciplines in project management, we plotted Figure 4-7 which shows the future availability and impact of each of the eight allied disciplines. By carefully considering Figure 4-7, we observe that the project management community expects that in the future (1) IT/IS and OB/HRM will have substantially more impact than availability of knowledge, (2) TECH/INNOV/NPD/R&D, STRATEGY/PPM, PERFORM/EVM, QM/6SIGMA/PI, and OR/DS/OM/SCM will have somewhat more impact than avail-

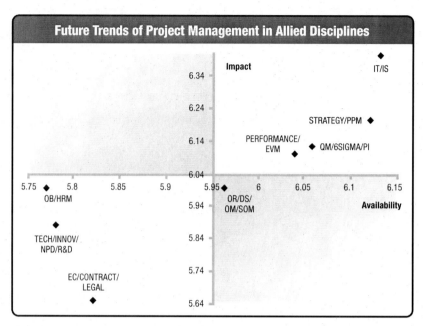

Figure 4-5   Future Trends of Project Management in Allied
             Disciplines

Low Availability, High Impact	High Availability, High Impact
None	PERFORMANCE/EVM QM/6SIGMA/PI STRATEGY/PPM IT/IS
Low Availability, Low Impact OB/HRM TECH/INNOV/NPD/R&D EC/CONTRACT/LEGAL	**High Availability, Low Impact** OR/DS/OM/SCM

Figure 4-6   Future Trends of Availability-Impact Matrix

ability of knowledge, and (3) EC/CONTRACT/LEGAL will have substantially more availability of knowledge than impact on project
management. These observations indicate that in general, there will
be more impact than availability of knowledge, call for further

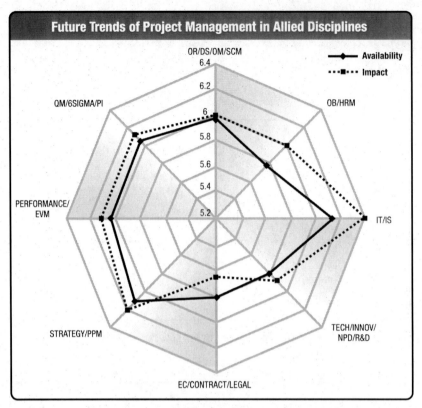

Figure 4-7   Comparison of Future Impact and Availability of
              Allied Disciplines

research and dissemination of knowledge in most of the allied disciplines, and highlight areas which are particularly expected to have more impact than availability of knowledge from the perspective of project management community.

Analysis clearly shows that all eight disciplines have an upward trend in terms of availability and impact starting from the 1960s to the future. In fact, Figures 4-3, 4-4, and 4-6 provide some thoughts by categorizing and dividing the eight disciplines into four quadrants by using values of availability and impact.

However, there are inherent limitations on analyzing and forecasting the future of the eight disciplines related to project management. Realizing that the values of current and future of the eight disciplines related to project management are simply relative to each other, we normalized the two sets of data (current and future) and overlapped the plots of current and future of the eight disciplines to visualize the trends and opportunities of the eight disciplines in the

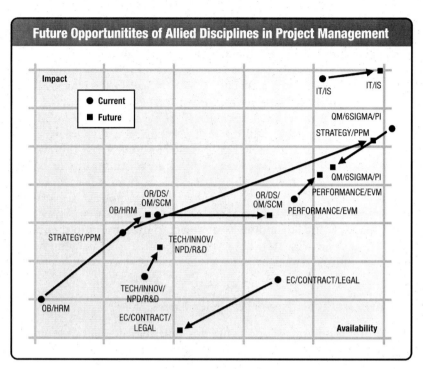

Figure 4-8   Future Opportunitites of Allied Disciplines in
              Project Management

	Availability		Impact	
Allied Disciplines	**Current**	**Future**	**Current**	**Future**
OR/DS/OM/SCM	Low	High	Same	Same
OB/HRM	Low	High	Low	High
IT/IS	Low	High	Low	High
TECH/INNOV/NPD/R&D	Low	High	Low	High
EC/CONTRACT/LEGAL	High	Low	High	Low
STRATEGY/PPM	Low	High	Low	High
PERFORMANCE/EVM	Low	High	Low	High
QM/6SIGMA/PI	High	Low	High	Low

Table 4-6   Future Trends of Allied Disciplines in Project
             Management

future as shown in Figure 4-8. This analysis provides us with clear and meaningful information to highlight research opportunities and impact of the allied disciplines as shown in Table 4-6.

The analysis indicates that STRATEGY/PPM, OB/HRM, IT/IS, PERFORMANCE/EVM, and TECH/INNOV/NPD/R&D would have more availability in knowledge and information and have greater impact in the future. EC/CONTRACT/LEGAL and QM/6SIGMA/PI would have less availability in knowledge and information and less impact in the future. OR/DS/OM/SCM showed that there would be more availability in knowledge and information but the impact will remain the same in the future. It is interesting to note that except for OR/DS/OM/SCM, current research publications in the top 18 management and business journals associate strongly with the impact of allied disciplines on project management in the future. This shows that research being published in top management and business journals may be setting the trends of impact on project management and its allied disciplines in the future.

4.4 Future Trends and Implications

4.4.1 Trends of Allied Disciplines and their Potential Impact on the Future of Project Management

More and more organizations are embracing project management practices and incorporating the allied disciplines into these practices to resolve complex management issues. Allied disciplines are becoming more sophisticated in their theories, tools, and applications and will continue to add value to project management concepts, theories, and applications. More collaboration among allied disciplines and project management will happen due to their proven efficiency and effectiveness of various disciplines. Project management and allied disciplines will continue to make recognizable contributions to the management community. Eventually, project management will be the language of good management practice as accounting is the language of business.

The availability of research in project management and its allied disciplines has exploded over the last 20 years. OB/HRM is a critical discipline in the project management world. So much of what organizations do is managing internal and external business and human resources and relationships. Fundamentally, project management today is more about people management than about task orientation. However, this trend of shifting from OR/DS/OM/SCM to OB/HRM has possibly reached its peak. IT/IS will continue to provide enhanced tools for project management, and will have a high impact in the future. As the IT/IS discipline matures, project management tools and techniques will continue to become available to general users, which makes it easier to implement project management principles.

PERFORMANCE/EVM and related methods for measuring project performance will grow more rapidly than today particularly due to governmental regulations requiring systematic cost/schedule evaluation in managing government projects. Relevant metrics in all of the allied disciplines and measurement activities will be critical to the performance of management, which will lead to enhanced probability of project success in the global economy.

STRATEGY/PPM and QM/6SIGMA/PI should have a growing impact on project management, as business strategies are developed and qualities are measured and analyzed to plan and implement effective project management. For many organizations, the biggest gains that they see come from adapting and implementing STRATEGY/PPM and QM/6SIGMA/PI.

TECH/INNOV/NPD/R&D and PERFORMANCE/EVM are poised to make major breakthroughs given the recent organizational interest and institutional determination on achieving project success. OR/DS/OM/SCM, PERFORMANCE/EVM, IT/IS, and TECH/INNOV/NPD/R&D will work together to deliver tools and techniques to allow the "science" of planning, scheduling, and cost control to function in a real project delivery environment.

In the future, project management as a discipline will be getting closer to the general management and organization theory fields because project management needs the theoretical advances that exist within these fields, and because management and organization theory need project management as projects are becoming an integral part of modern management in a number of industries and sectors. The trends of the allied disciplines and their potential impact on project management will depend on the successful integration of organizational strategies. In other words, if organizations embrace the alignment of allied disciplines and project management, then the impact on project management will be fully recognized and project management should become an integral component of mainstream management thought and practice. Obviously, the allied disciplines will bring great value to project management as the interdisciplinary concepts and practices become more widely used and understood by practicing project managers and by operational, general, and executive management.

4.4.2 Trends of Allied Disciplines and Project Management

Project management will become more flexible and dynamic to meet increasing expectations. It will move closer toward OB/HRM with access to the latest information systems and knowledge. Dealing with people, conflicts, team building, knowledge sharing, and communication will be determinants of good project management. Working in virtual project teams, understanding the global business environment, and using state-of-the-art technology systems will be applied to every project. Project management will become more multidisciplinary and flexible in adopting tools from other disciplines and become a generally acknowledged management discipline.

Project management will be more advanced to embrace and accommodate various characteristics of allied disciplines. As the allied disciplines evolve with new business trends, project management will follow these trends as they are closely related. Project management will eventually incorporate relevant parts of allied disciplines, and project management will formally recognize various disciplines and apply them as part of the project management knowledge base. Project management would be seen as the conduit of many organizational activities and will be partners with the different allied disciplines to achieve the strategic goals of the organization. Project management should be the driving force to implement new initiatives and processes. As these disciplines become more widely used there will be more management interest and awareness of their value.

Project management has a lot to learn from allied disciplines. The practice of project management in different disciplines will increase the overall awareness of project management in many fields. The growing knowledge base will formalize the discipline of project management, increase the effectiveness, and influence new project management practices. Project management will be a recognized career path, with practitioners capable of moving to executive management levels. Relevant knowledge developed in the allied disciplines will be integrated into project management processes as opposed to being considered as part of related disciplines. Requirements and advances of allied disciplines should drive development of new thoughts, processes, and procedures in project management.

Corporations will not be searching for the less expensive alternatives and resources as much as they will be seeking professionals with multidisciplinary experience (i.e., behavioral sciences, quality management, project management, etc.). The project management profession will be much more about collaboration rather than about control. The mutual influence of these disciplines and project management will mean that the knowledge available from each of them will be readily applied, and organizations will utilize project management as the agent of change and continual improvement.

From the research standpoint, it is exciting to see how project management will be affected. From the integration of management fields new and interesting knowledge may emerge for the science, art, and practice of project management. Theoretical developments give academic scholars theories to work with. The actual application of project management in a real life situation could be quite different from that of theory. Having meaningful theories to work with will assist the project management community in implementing new knowledge and techniques in the field.

4.4.3 The Project Management Community's Mindset and the Trends of Allied Disciplines

Project management should strengthen its philosophical foundations to include ideas in the sociological, cultural, political, and spiritual realms. The project management community should be engaged in adapting new ideas and changes and look at how social networks and collaborative thinking work in project management. The project management community must understand that the allied disciplines are needed and must embrace and apply them as part of project management. To do so, the project management community should be engaged in acquiring knowledge and participating in major activities of the allied disciplines to better understand the emerging and promising practices for future project endeavors. Project management should never forget human aspects such as trust, teamwork, and pride.

Trends and strategies will continue to evolve as project management becomes the norm. It will be an ever-changing field where highly skilled, multifaceted project managers will be in high demand. To ensure that project management flourishes, there is a need for conducting research, asking questions, and developing intellectual resources. Project management needs to revamp itself. The mindset should move toward a collaborative attitude rather than being separate from all others. Each of the allied disciplines should be respected for its knowledge, expertise, and wisdom. The role of project management should be viewed as the focal point of information gathering and dissemination to other areas of related disciplines.

The emerging generation of project management researchers has a very open mindset to the integration of knowledge from allied fields. The European Academy of Management (EURAM) Conferences, the International Research Network on Organizing by Projects (IRNOP) Conferences, and the Academy of Management (AOM) Professional Development Workshops and symposia are positive signs of this progress. The project management community should focus on enhancing its capabilities in both the hard and soft disciplines. It should embrace all research that improves the interaction of people to people, people to technology, as well as technology to technology.

Project management practitioners and researchers need to increase their leadership and presence in industry through continued education and information sharing. They should lead the way in driving the implementation of business strategies with knowledge of STRATEGY/PPM and QM/6Sigma/PI as well as better understanding of behavioral issues and complexity of the project world. An open mindset is particularly needed. The project management profession is continuously evolving, so the project management community should be receptive to new ideas, and also sensitive to the yearning of the public and professional community so as to model project management practices to meet their expectations. The greatest suggestion we can make is to aggressively educate more business professionals on project management as a discipline.

4.5 Thoughts from Project Management Scholars and Practitioners

4.5.1 Thoughts from Scholar A

The impact of decision sciences on project management was high until the 1960s. Project management had its genesis in operations research, and until the 1960s its genesis in operations research was high. Various research activities done in Vienna, Austria, during the 1970s were in critical path analysis. However, since the 1970s the relative importance, knowledge, and research in this area have been decreasing. Research in HRM on project management started in the 1970s, and has been growing since then. EVM impact on project management was low in the 1970s and 1980s but has been growing since then. Innovation within project management was not strong in the 1970s, because project management was basically used as a tool for the measurement of innovation. Innovation and R&D have not been hugely impacted by project management. The impact prior to the 1980s was low because project management was associated with construction. IT and Innovation/R&D impact on project management started in the early 1960s when IBM used project management in the development of its products. However, an appreciable growth in the impact of innovation/R&D on project management was witnessed from the 1980s. In the late 1980s, the impact of organizational strategy on project management was low but has shown an appreciable increase in the late 1990s and now. Quality was low until the early 1980s, and has been growing since then.

Project management practices can enhance the strategic marketing capacity of organizations. However, project management practices encourage task-focused behavior because of the nature of projects being driven by time, and project managers tend to be more task-focused to get projects delivered on time. Also, the transition from project managers to senior managers is always easier in engineering companies than in other companies.

In the future project management will be more sophisticated in that it will become less task-focused and become more people-focused. One future research topic is the well-being of project managers. Project management needs to be recognized in the management faculty and accorded an equal status with other traditional management sciences disciplines. In the future, project management should be a division in the Academy of Management. To do so, project management professionals and academic communities need to sell themselves better.

4.5.2 Thoughts from Scholar B

If the word gets out about research in project management, then it would not be long before project management is established as an area in management science, as in the case of stochastic modeling, which emerged as a quite relevant set of topics and areas in the last 10 to 15 years. If researchers become aware of the types of problems that arise in project management, then there will probably be more interest in the academic community. It is a matter of time. Operations research is true to the modeling paradigm. Computer science/IT is a new area. The areas being studied such as strategy, performance, IT, HRM, and quality are very similar to those relevant to operations management. The question is whether researchers in operations management have recognized problems in project management. There is as much potential for developing new theories in project management as has been seen in other focus areas. A focused area is more likely to be researched. Practitioners are focused on broader problems. Contributions from academics are in specific areas. Relevance of some of these topics is important. There are challenges in taking project management to the mainstream.

Academic outlets may trail practice. It is very rare that academics lead practice, especially in social sciences, because we do not have access to the context in which theories are being applied, as opposed to say physics or chemistry in which research can be conducted successfully in research and academic institutions. If problems are generic enough, then they do not lose much (or a lot) by taking them out of their context. Arguments about relevance will continue as with many academic disciplines. Since this is a general issue in management research.

4.5.3 Thoughts from Scholar C

Project management is an important skill to run IT/IS projects, which could be different from building a bridge. Planning, scheduling, and risk management are very critical for the success of IT/IS projects and for the success of the company. We are recommending that more and more students in IT/IS take a project management course. In the new curriculum, project management is one of the required courses at the graduate level. People make a case that undergraduate students may not appreciate project management, but I think some of them would. They can use project management skills at least to manage their studies but also to survive in the new world. I usually recommend that students take a project management course. One of my students did not. He moved on to be a project manager and then a Chief Information Officer. He came to speak in my class and his recommendation to students was: Take a project management course!

Given the bad reputation of IT/IS projects of going past their schedules and exceeding their budgets, we must try project management. What do we have to lose? IT/IS project management is more critical because the project manager needs to deal with diversity, which is a critical part of project management education. Now, there are fewer women in IT/IS. More diversity would be benefical in IT/IS and in project management if team members were to use their strengths such as communications and peacemaking in their project teams. There are two IT/IS journals in the FT40 list. Two other relevant journals are *Journal of the Association for Information Systems* and *Communications of the Association for Information Systems*. I have not seen much research on project management in the IT/IS area in these journals, but I believe that this is a fruitful research area. IT/IS is still struggling as an academic discipline in some people's eyes. Many people still think that IT/IS is fixing one's machine, installing software, or helping with a spreadsheet.

4.5.4 Thoughts from Scholar D

There are very interesting developments in project management in comparison to traditional management. Based on industrial economy, we traditionally think in terms of managing a big, costly factory with yearly model changes or managing a hotel, or managing a facility, and so on. However, products are becoming obsolete faster. So, we find that we need to construct a new factory, a new building, satellites, network towers, an enterprise resource planning system, and other change projects. Writing an article is a smaller project. For companies, it is a larger model of management replacing traditional management. Software can be a great aid to project management to help with coordination. It is good to have technology available. Projects are becoming an electronic era phenomenon.

Thomas Friedman (2005) in *The World is Flat* speaks of a platform and discusses globalization of countries (1492–1800), companies (1800–2000), and individuals (2000 and beyond). This involves the Internet, outsourcing, and collaboration beyond the boundaries of the organization. Academic globalization is allowing scholars to collaborate on a variety of projects. The academic world is undergoing interesting changes. IT is a preamble and we are now starting to utilize it. Once software is developed, people around the world can start using it. More and more people get involved and they create a new world. We are just beginning to use this platform and have not thought through various implications. We need to keep these huge changes in mind. Projects are a new direction from the manufacturing perspective of management. The increasing use of English flattens the world and enhances collaboration among multinational teams in projects. There is an ideological shift dissolving political, government, union, and other differences for greater economic prosperity. Many Eastern European countries are moving towards homogenization and internationalization to join the European Union. Similar changes could affect the U.S. Global warming, sea level rise, and carbon emissions will have a significant impact on major cities and regions of the world by the end of this century. Discussion of these issues is just beginning. This will result in big technology and infrastructure projects within decades. Better project managers will be needed for these projects. Project management is the way to go.

4.5.5 Thoughts from Scholar E

There is a lot more interest in project management in business and government and the academic community is responding to that. There is more awareness of project management in the academic community. Decision sciences and operations research are moving towards practical issues, focusing more on practice, and obtaining ideas from it. The organizations with which I interface are dealing with project management more. Decision sciences and operations research will follow along although they are not providing much leadership in project management. Interest in decision sciences and operations research is steady but not growing whereas interest in project management is increasing more. Probably decision sciences and operations research will play a smaller role in project management in the future.

There is a potential for an increased interest in project management in the future. However, the academic community is not providing much leadership in that area.

4.5.6 Thoughts from Practitioner A

Project management has always been a product of Operations Research, and Operations Research has waned in recent times. EVM and Six Sigma are important tools in project management. Six Sigma is important, however, it is all about getting the right measurement of the process. It has gone somewhat too far such that government and the private sector have gone measurement crazy. Portfolio/Program Management will become more important in the future. The next generation of project managers will have a more profound project management experience and probably portfolio management experience. Integrative skill is a very good skill needed to be developed by all project and portfolio managers. The ability to integrate all the facets of a project or group of projects to ascertain their cross-impact is a very much needed skill among project/portfolio managers. Project management is highly strategic because it has always been a means to an end and not an end itself, so the output of a project is the starting point for achieving the outcome of a business and the outcome is basically what is strategic. Once a corporate strategy has been determined, project/program management is the best tool to help organizations gain some kind of discipline in the achievement of its strategic objectives.

For any organization to survive, there must be a value that is represented at all levels of the organization. In the future there will be more organizations striving to be more ethical. There will be more corporate social responsibility all of which will have impact on the nature of projects. As project management becomes more of the transformational way of moving forward, ethics and corporate social responsibility will be integrated in all facets of project management practice. In the future, project management will affect everything.

4.5.7 Thoughts from Practitioner B

It is going to be a project-based world in the future that will respond to increasing complexity, requirements for accountability, globalization, and the need for talent and competence. The project management discipline is needed to deal with challenges in a more complex, uncertain world. Project management is the next stage of management and leadership to meet the demands for efficiency and successful outcomes. It is difficult to think of aspects of management that do not need project management. The world is very different and projects are very different. Knowledge and skills need to be adapted to grow the project management field effectively. Theory and practice need to adapt to provide the next generation of leadership and management. There are complex, multi-directional forces that shape government, industry, and universities. Aspects of all of these forces need to be adapted to meet the challenges of project management.

Decisions are the root of success. The OB/HRM dimension is so obvious that it gets ignored. Human capital needs to adapt to a project world and its leadership requirements. IT/IS/software drives so much although it may appear separate from the mission and projects, and it needs to adapt. Innovation and R&D is a key, very exiting area. Technology and resources need to be adapted. In the engineering/construction area, project management established itself and needs to adapt to the next stage. Strategy and portfolio management require leadership and constitute the majority of the next pushes in organizations. Cost and schedule performance are essential drivers. There are important advances in quality and Six Sigma that are needed to run projects successfully. As far as other areas, it would be well to separate out leadership. Senior leaders/ executives separate themselves from project management. In training the workforce, they see project management to be as important at lower levels. High-performing teams need leadership which requires OB/HRM and strategy. Government needs to be able to identify cost and respond in a timely manner to major disasters. Another area is knowledge management, which ensures that processes and standards are the basis for training, supports team focused learning, and supports community. It improves the use of resources to meet challenges and provide solutions. Wiki/bloggers provide a collective community for project solutions and awareness. It is going to be a project world. If something is important it will be done in a project mode. Project management needs to keep evolving and adapting and not be deterred or locked-in.

4.5.8 Thoughts from Practitioner C

Projects go into the hole because managers cannot understand the risk. An example of that is the Airbus A380 plane which was behind schedule. It led to billions of dollars of losses and also to the termination of two CEOs. One has to follow up when developing a new project. Risk management could have been applied to understanding the problems and issues as well as coming up with proper mitigation strategies. In any given project, mitigation strategies, as well as protection techniques that are suitable for the given risk, tie into the statistical probability. Companies want to have proper risk management strategies and that will help them achieve good financial goals, improve their working performance, ensure corporate governance (such as how much money has been spent and maintain an audit trail), as well as determine if and whether the project will be finished on time.

4.6 Future Recommendations and Conclusions

4.6.1 Impact of Project Management on Allied Disciplines in the Future

Project management is the integration and application of the allied disciplines. Project management can impact the allied disciplines by embracing them and incorporating them. Different disciplines are already incorporating project management into their thoughts and processes. Project management will be seen as an overall coordinator of the disciplines involved and will be infused into other disciplines. As allied disciplines see their outputs increasingly appreciated and adapted by project management, these disciplines will do more to remain relevant to project management and other disciplines. Allied disciplines will become part of project management—not separate disciplines. Some will become obsolete and some will be integrated under the project management umbrella. Project management will be looking into a flexible means to implement various theories from allied disciplines. This will continue into the future.

Project management will have great impact if industries understand the significance of what will happen if they use good project management in their business practices. Project management should assist with decision making from an executive level on down, throughout the entire organization. As more industries rely on quick changes in response to market demands, more industries will rely on project work to accomplish their goals. Executives will be looking for project management tools and methodologies to help increase project success rates. Project management tools will become more common to other industries. Project management will continue to evolve so that the impact of accomplishments, quality, and cost on projects will create a need for greater analytical tools to measure and visualize progress.

Project management has and will continue to have a tremendous impact on the allied disciplines. As these disciplines continue to find ways to be more efficient in implementing projects, they will continue to adopt project management methodologies and principles to control projects. Project management will have to consistently improve on its methodologies and find ways of improving and doing things more effectively. Project management will push the advancement and applications of areas like quality enhancement, human resources, team work, politics, research and development, information systems and knowledge management. Allied disciplines will utilize project management to grow beyond their traditional strong holds.

4.6.2 Project Management as a Discipline in the Future

Being multi-disciplinary in nature, project management will have a huge impact in the future. Project management will be the accepted way of getting work done in a flexible, outsourced, and projectized environment. Use of IT/IS will enable project managers to plan, manage, and control global projects in a virtual environment. The future of project management is already being written in the open source movement.

Virtual self-organizing and self-managed teams are likely to perform better than explicitly managed teams. The social networking phenomenon will assist in this and collaborative management will be the key. Project management will be viewed as 'business as usual' in the future. Corporations will be concerned with morale and employee development, due to the fact that project managers must be able to motivate and develop themselves and others in the fast-paced project management environment. Employees will have to be extremely well rounded and have project management skills as a requirement.

There will be more acceptance and recognition for the project management discipline. Organizations will come to the realization that project management is directly related to achieving strategic goals. Successful project management should be strategic and business oriented for output of products and services as compared to a high degree of process-oriented practices as we see today. Eventually, project management will become commonplace or the "norm" in organizations. Project management will become the future of doing business effectively, efficiently, and profitably, and will remain as a people-oriented discipline, especially with the new wave of global competition looming on the horizon. More effort and emphasis will be placed on the successful management of the portfolio of projects as opposed to one individual project at a time. This will require better use of OB/HRM and communications within the organization.

The fact that project management can be widely accepted and applied in today's industry and government depends to a great extent on the promotion of project management by the project management community. Project management is undergoing a transition to being considered a professional discipline. The future of project management looks optimistic, based on the need of every organization to adapt and improve constantly. Project management will provide the means to organizations to implement continual improvement. Project management is the current wave of global business, and based on this standpoint, project management will become a discipline and a profession of prestige in the business world. Eventually, project management will be an exciting knowledge area with solid theory where practitioners and academics can meet, where theory and practice can be co-produced.

CHAPTER 5

References

Abbott, A. (1988). *The system of professions: an essay on the division of expert labor*. Chicago: University of Chicago Press.

Abudayyeh, O., Dibert-DeYoung, A., & Jaselskis, E. (2004). Analysis of trends in construction research: 1985–2002. *Journal of Construction Engineering and Management*, 130, 433–439.

Academy of Management. (2007). Retrieved on October 23, 2007 from http://www.aomonline.org/aom.asp?page_ID=36.

Adminstrative Science Quarterly. (2007). Retrieved on October 23, 2007 from http://www.johnson.cornell.edu/publications/asq/description.html.

AOM Journal. (2007). Retrieved on October 23, 2007 from http://www.aom.pace.edu/amjnew/.

AOM Perspectives. (2007). Retrieved on October 23, 2007 from http://journals.aomonline.org/amp/.

AOM Review. (2007). Retrieved on October 23, 2007 from http://www.aom.pace.edu/amr/.

Bain, G. (1990). A vocational vortex. *The Times Higher Education Supplement*, February 23, 13.

Bain, G. S. (1992). Blackett memorial lecture: The future of management education. Journal *of the Operational Research Society*, 43(6), 557–561.

Banker, R. D., & Slaughter, S. A. (2000). The moderating effects of structure on volatility and complexity in software enhancement. *Information Systems Research*, 11(3), 219.

Barman, S., Hanna, M. D., & LaForge, R. W. (2001). Perceived relevance and quality of POM journals: a decade later. *Journal of Operations Management*, 19(3), 367–385.

Barman, S., Tersine, R. J., & Buckley, M. R. (1991). An empirical assessment of the perceived relevance and quality of POM-related journals by academicians. *Journal of Operations Management, 10*(2), 194–212.

Betts, M., & Lansley, P. (1995) *International Journal of Project Management:* A review of the first ten years. *International Journal of Project Management, 12*(4), 207–217.

Bunch, J. F. S. (2003). Connecting the dots: Aligning projects with objectives in unpredictable times. *Academy of Management Executive, 17*(4), 157–159.

Burack, E. H. (1967). Industrial management in advanced production systems: Some theoretical concepts and preliminary findings. *Administrative Science Quarterly, 12*(3), 479.

Burns, L. R. (1989). Matrix management in hospitals: Testing theories of matrix structure and development. *Administrative Science Quarterly, 34*(3), 349.

Butler, J., Morrice, D. J., & Mullarkey, P. W. (2001). A multiple attribute utility theory approach to ranking and selection. *Management Science, 47*(6), 800–816.

California Management Review. (2007). Retrieved on October 23, 2007 from http://cmr.berkeley.edu/submission_guidelines.html.

Carter, E. E. (1971). The behavioral theory of the firm and top-level corporate decisions. *Administrative Science Quarterly, 16*(4), 413.

Cascio, W. F. (2000). Managing a virtual workplace. *Academy of Management Executive, 14*(3), 81–90.

Charnes, A., & Cooper, W. W. (1957). Management models and industrial applications of linear programming. *Management Science, 4*(1), 38–91.

Cianni, M., & Wnuck, D. (1997). Individual growth and team enhancement: moving toward a new model of career development. *Academy of Management Executives, 11*(1), 105–115.

Cook, D. L., & Granger, J. C. (1976). Current status of project management instruction in American colleges and universities. *Academy of Management Journal, 19*(2), 323–328.

Corbett, C. J., & Van Wassenhove, L. N. (1993). The natural drift: What happened to operations research? *Operations Research, 41*, 423–455.

Crawford, L., Pollack, J., & England, D. (2006) Uncovering the trends in project management: journal emphasis over the last 10 years. *International Journal of Project Management, 24*, 175–184.

Crowston, W. B. (1971). Models for project management. *Sloan Management Review; 12*(3), 25–42.

Crowston, W., & Thompson, G. L. (1967). Decision CPM: A Method for Simultaneous Planning, Scheduling, and Control of Projects. *Operations Research, 15*(3), 407–426.

Delionback, L. M., & Meinhart, W. A. (1968). Project management: An incentive contracting decision model. *Academy of Management Journal, 11*(4), 427–434.

Dillon, R. D., Paté-Cornell, E. M., & Guikema, S. D. (2003). Programmatic risk analysis for critical engineering systems under tight resource constraints. *Operations Research, 51*(3), 354.

Dunne, E. J., Jr., Stahl, M. J., & Melhart, L. J., Jr. (1978). Influence source of project and functional managers in matrix organizations. *Academy of Management Journal, 21*(1), 135–140.

Engwall, M., & Svensson, C. (2001). Cheetah Teams. *Harvard Business Review, 79*(2), 20–21.

Fichman, R. G. (2004). Real options and IT platform adoption: Implications for theory and practice. *Information Systems Research, 15*(2), 132–154.

Fleming, Q. W., & Koppelman, J. M. (2003). What's your project's real price tag? *Harvard Business Review, 81*(9), 20–22.

Forrester, J., & Drexler, A. B. (1999). A model for team-based organizational performance. *Academy of Management Executive, 13*(3), 36–49.

Franks Report (1963). British business schools. London: British Institute of Management.

Friedman, T. L. (2005). *The world is flat: Brief history of the twenty-first century.* New York: Farrar, Straus and Giroux.

Gaddis, P. O. (1959). The project manager. *Harvard Business Review, 37*(3), 89–97.

Gerwin, D. (2004). Coordinating new product development in strategic alliances. *Academy of Management Review, 29*(2), 241–257.

Gerwin, D., & Ferris, J. S. (2004). Organizing new product development projects in strategic alliances. *Organization Science, 15*(1), 22–37.

Goh, C.H., Holsapple, C.W., Johnson, L.E., and Tanner, J.R. (1997). Evaluating and classifying POM journals, *Journal of Operations Management, 15*(2), May, 123–138.

Goodman, R. A. (1967). Ambiguous authority definition in project management. *Academy of Management Journal, 10*(4), 13–18.

Gottschalg, O., & Zollo, M. (2007). Interest alignment and competitive advantage. *Academy of Management Review, 32*(2), 418–437.

Guinan, P. J., Cooprider, J. G., & Faraj, S. (1998). Enabling software development team performance during requirements definition: A behavioral versus technical Sloan approach. *Information Systems Research, 9*(2), 101–125.

Gustafsson, J., & Salo, A. (2005). Contingent portfolio programming for the management of risky projects. *Operations Research*, 53(6), 946–995.

Gutierrez, G., & Paul, A. (2000). Analysis of the effects of uncertainty, risk-pooling, and subcontracting mechanisms on project performance. *Operations Research*, 48(6), 927.

Harvard Business Review. (2007). Retrieved on October 23, 2007 from http://harvardbusinessonline.hbsp.harvard.edu/b02/en/common/util_contact_guidelines_hbr.jhtml.

Haas, M. R. (2006). Knowledge gathering, team capabilities, and project performance in challenging work environments. *Management Science*, 52(8), 1170–1184.

Hodgetts, R. M. (1968). Leadership techniques in project organization. *Academy of Management Journal*, 11(2), 211–219.

Hoffman, G. H. (1982). Project cost control: Dynamic risk analysis of randomly ordered sequential decisions under uncertainty. *Interfaces*, 12(3), 45–51.

Howell, R. A. (1968). Multiproject control. *Harvard Business Review*, 46(2), 63–70.

IEEE TEM. (2007). Retrieved on October 23, 2007 from http://ieeexplore.ieee.org/xpl/RecentIssue.jsp?punumber=17.

Information Systems Research. (2007). Retrieved on October 23, 2007 from http://isr.journal.informs.org/misc/about.dtl.

INFORMS. (2007). Retrieved on October 23, 2007 from http://www.informs.org/index.php?c=7&kat=ABOUT.

Interfaces. (2007). Retrieved on October 23, 2007 from http://www.informs.org/site/Interfaces/.

Ireland, R. D., Reutzel, C. R., & Webb, J. W. (2005). From the editors: Entrepreneurship research in AMJ: What has been published, and what might the future hold? *Academy of Management Journal*, 48(4), 556–564.

Jain, H. K., Tanniru, M. R., & Fazlollahi, B. (1991). MCDM approach for generating and evaluating alternatives in requirement analysis. *Information Systems Research*, 2(3), 223–239.

Journal of Operations Management. (2007). Retrieved on October 23, 2007 from http://www.elsevier.com/locate/jom.

Karl, K. A. (1999). Mastering virtual teams. *Academy of Management Executive*, 13(3), 118–119.

Keefer, D. L., Kirkwood, C. W., & Corner, J. L. (2004). Perspective on decision analysis applications, 1990–2001. *Decision Analysis*, 1, 5–24.

Kessler, E. H., & Bierly, P. E., III. (2001). Vasa Syndrome: Insights from a 17th century new-product disaster. *Academy of Management Executives*, 15(3), 80–91.

Kirsch, L. J. (1996). The management of complex tasks in organizations: Controlling the Systems development process. *Organization Science, 7*(1), 1–21.

Kunreuther, H. (1969). Extension of Bowman's Theory on managerial decision-making. *Management Science; 15*(8), B415–B439.

Jassawalla, A. R., & Sashittal, H. C. (2002). Cultures that support production-innovation processes. *Academy of Management Executive, 16*(3), 42–54.

Larson, E. W., & Gobeli, D. H. (1991). Application of project management by small businesses to develop new products and services. *Journal of Small Business Management, 29*(2), 30–41.

Lee, Z., Gosain, S., & Im, I. (1999). Topics of interest in IS: Evolution of themes and differences between research and practice. *Information & Management, 336*, 233–246.

Leifer, R., O'Connor, G. C., & Rice, M. (2001). Implementing radical innovation in mature firms. *Academy of Management Executive, 15*(3), 102–113.

Li, H., Bingham, J. B., & Umphress, E. E. (2007). Fairness from the top: Perceived procedural justice and collaborative problem solving in new product development. *Organization Science, 18*(2), 200–216.

Liao, S. (2005). Technology management methodologies and applications: a literature review from 1995 to 2003. *Technovation, 25*, 381–292.

Linton, J. D. (2006). Ranking of technology and innovation management journals. *Technovation, 26*, 2885–2887.

Linton, J. D., & Thongpapanl, N. (2004). Perspective: Ranking the technology innovation management journals. *Journal of Product Innovation Management, 21*, 123–139.

Long Range Planning. (2007). Retrieved on October 23, 2007 from http://www.lrp.ac/.

Malhotra, A., Majchrzak, A., & Benson, R. (2007). Leading virtual teams. *Academy of Management Perspectives, 21*(1), 60–70.

Management Science. (2007). Retrieved on October 23, 2007 from http://mansci.journal.informs.org/misc/about.dtl.

Mankins, M. C., & Steele, R. (2005). Turning great strategy into great performance. *Harvard Business Review, 83*(7/8), 64–72.

Maxfield, M. W. (1981). Sequencing and scheduling in real time—quickly. *Interfaces, 11*(3), 40–43.

Macfarlane, B., & Ottewill, R. (Eds.) (2001). *Effective learning and teaching in business and management*. London: Routledge.

Merino, T. G., Pereira do Carmo, L., & Alvarez, V. S. (2006). 25 Years of Technovation: characteristics and evolution of the journal. *Technovation, 26*, 1303–1316.

Middleton, C. J. (1967). How to set up a project organization. *Harvard Business Review, 45*(2), 73–82.

Mihm, J., Loch, C., & Huchzermeier, A. (2003). Problem-solving oscillations in complex engineering projects. *Management Science, 49*(6), 733–750.

Miles, R. E., Snow, C. S., Mathews, J. A., Miles, G., & Coleman, H.J., Jr. (1997). Organizing in the knowledge age: Anticipating the cellular form. *Academy of Management Executive, 11*(4), 7–20.

Miller, R. W. (1962). How to plan and control with PERT. *Harvard Business Review, 40*(2), 93–104.

MIS Quarterly. (2007). Retrieved on October 23. 2007 from http://www.misq.org/archived.

Mitchell, V. L., & Nault, B. R. (2007). Cooperative planning, uncertainty, and managerial control in concurrent design. *Management Science, 53*(3), 375–389.

Northcraft, G. B. & Wolf, G. (1984). Dollars, sense, and sunk costs: a life cycle model of resource allocation decisions. *Academy of Management Review, 9*(2), 225.

Nuffield. (2007). Retrieved on October 12, 2007 from http://www.nuffield.ox.ac.uk/general/lordnuffield.aspx

Olson, J. E. (2005) Top-25 business-school professors rate journals in operations management and related fields. *Interfaces, 35*(4), 323–338.

O'Connor, G. C., Rice, M. P., Peters, L., & Veryzer, R. W. (2003). Managing interdisciplinary, longitudinal research teams: extending grounded theory-building methodologies. *Organization Science, 14*(4), 353–373.

O'Hear, A. (1988). *The element of fire: Science, art and the human world.* London: Routledge.

Operations Research. (2007). Retrieved on October 23, 2007 from http://or.journal.informs.org/misc/about.dtl.

Organization Science. (2007). Retrieved on October 23, 2007 from http://orgsci.journal.informs.org/misc/about.dtl.

Ormerod, R. & Kiossis, I. (1997). OR/MS publications: extension of the analysis of U.S. flagship journals to the United Kingdom. *Operations Research, 45,* 178–187.

Palvia, P., Pinjain, P., & Sibley, E. H. (2007). A profile of information system research published in *Information & Management. Information & Management, 44,* 1–11.

Pitsis, T., Clegg, S. R., Marosszeky, M., & Rura-Polley, T. (2003). Constructing the Olympic dream: A future perfect strategy of project management. *Organization Science, 14*(5), 574–590.

Prasad, S., & Babbar, S. (2000). International operations management research. *Journal of Operations Management, 18*(2), 209–247.

Project Management Institute (PMI®). (2004). *A guide to the project management body of knowledge (PMBOK® Guide)* – Third Edition. Newtown Square, PA: Project Management Institute.

Price, M. J. & Chen, E. E. (1993). Total quality management in a small, high-technology company. *California Management Review, 35*(3), 96.

Reisman, A., & Kirschnick, F. (1994). The devolution of OR/MS: implications from a statistical content analysis of papers in flagship journals. *Operations Research, 42*, 577–588.

Ranganathan, C., & Brown, C. V. (2006). ERP investments and the market value of firms: Toward an understanding of influential ERP project variables. *Information Systems Research, 17*(2), 145–161.

Reisman, A. (1994). Technology management: A brief Review of the last 40 years and some thoughts on its future. *IEEE Transactions of Engineering Management, 41*(4), 342–346.

Rogers, J. (1958). A computational approach to the economic lot scheduling problem. *Management Science, 4*(3), 264–291.

Roman, D. D. (1964). Project management recognizes R&D performance. *Academy of Management Journal, 7*(1), 7–20.

Santiago, L. P., & Vakili, P. (2005). On the value of flexibility in R&D projects. *Management Science, 51*(8), 1206–1218.

Schussel, G., & Price, S. (1970). A case history in optimum inventory scheduling. *Operations Research, 18*(1), 1–23.

Scott, S. G., & Einstein, W. O. (2001). Strategic performance appraisal in team-based organizations. *Academy of Management Executive, 15*(2), 107–116.

Shenhar, A. J. (2001). One size does not fit all projects: Exploring classical contingency domains. *Management Science, 47*(3), 394–414.

Sivaramakrishnan, K., & Gopal, A. (2003). Contracts in offshore development. *Management Science, 49*(12), 1671–1683.

Sloan Management Review. (2007). Retrieved on October 23, 2007 from http://sloanreview.mit.edu/smr/authoring/.

Söderlund, J. (2004) Building theories of project management: Past research, questions for the future. *International Journal of Project Management, 22*, 183–191.

Soteriou, A. C., Hadjinicola, G. C., & Patsia, K. (1999). Assessing production and operations management related journals: The European perspective. *Journal of Operations Management, 17*(2), 225–238.

Strategic Management Journal. (2007). Retrieved on October 23, 2007 from http://www3.interscience.wiley.com/cgi-bin/jabout/2144/ProductInformation.html.

Szmerekovsky, J. G. (2005). The impact of contractor behavior on the client's payment-scheduling problem. *Management Science, 51*(4), 629–640.

Thamhain, H. J., & Gemmil, G. R. (1974). Influence of project managers: some project performance correlates. *Academy of Management Journal, 17*(2), 216–224.

Themistocleous, G., & Wearne, S. H. (2000). Project management topic coverage in journals, *International Journal of Project Management, 31*(2), 7–11.

Townsend, A. M., DeMarie, S. M., & Hendrickson, A. R. (1998). Virtual teams: Technology and the workplace of the future. *Academy of Management Executive, 13*(3), 17–29.

Vanhoucke, M., & Demeulemeester, E. (2001). On maximizing the net present value of a project under renewable resource constraints. *Management Science, 47*(8), 1113–1121.

Vazsonyi, A. (1982). Computer-supported Gedanken experiments. *Interfaces, 12*(4), 34–41.

Vokurka, R. J. (1996). The relative importance of journals used in operations management research: A citation analysis. *Journal of Operations Management, 14*(4), 345–355.

Wasil, E.A., & Assad, A. A. (1988). Project management on the PC: software, applications, and trends. *Interfaces, 18*(2), 75–84.

Wilemon, D. L., & Cicero, J. P. (1970). Project manager: Anomalies and ambiguities. *Academy of Management Journal, 13*(3), 269–282.

Winter, M., & Smith, C. (2006). Rethinking Project Management (EPSRC Network 2004–2006). Final Report. Retrieved September 28, 2007, from http://www.mace.manchester.ac.uk/project/research/management/rethinkpm/pdf/final_report.pdf

Zangill, W. I. (1966). A deterministic multiproduct, multifacility production and inventory model. *Operations Research, 14*(3), 486–507.

APPENDIX A

18 Top Management and Business Journal Articles List

Academy of Management Perspectives

Ref. #	Class. Code	Year	Journal Articles
18	2	2007	Malhotra, A., Majchrzak, A., & Benson, R. (2007). Leading Virtual Teams. *Academy of Management Perspectives,* (21)1, 60–70.
17	2	2004	Webber, S. S., & Torti, M. T. (2007). Project Managers Doubling as Client Account Executives. *Academy of Management Executive,* 18(1), 60–71.
16	6	2003	Bunch, J. F. S. (2003). Connecting The Dots: Aligning Projects with Objectives in Unpredictable Times. *Academy of Management Executive,* 17(4), 157–159.
15	2	2002	Shipp, S. (2002). Soul: A Book for A Few Dozen Computer Scientist. *Academy of Management Executive,* 16(4), 64–68.
14	2	2002	Jassawalla, A. R., & Sashittal. H. C. (2002). Cultures that Support Production-Innovation Processes. *Academy of Management Executive,* 16(3), 42–54.
13	2,6	2001	Kessler, E. H., & Bierly, P. E., III. (2001). Vasa Syndrome: Insights from a 17th Century New-Product Disaster. *Academy of Management Executive,* 15(3), 80–91.
12	6	2001	Leifer, R., O'Connor, G. C., & Rice, M. (2001). Implementing Radical Innovation in Mature Firms. *Academy of Management Executive,* 15(3), 102–113.
11	2	2001	Scott, S. G., & Einstein, W. O. (2001). Strategic Performance Appraisal in Team-Based Organizations. *Academy of Management Executive,* 15(2), 107–116.
10	2	2000	Cascio, W. F. (2000). Managing a Virtual Workplace. *Academy of Management Executive,* 14(3), 81–90.
9	2	1999	Forrester, R., & Drexler, A. B.. (1999). A Model for Team-based Organizational Performance. *Academy of Management Executive,* 13(3), 36–49.
8	2	1999	Karl, K. A. (1999). Mastering Virtual Teams. *Academy of Management Executive,* 13(3), 118–119.

(continued next page)

7	2,3	1998	Townsend, A. M., DeMarie, S. M., & Hendrickson, A. R. (1998). Virtual Teams: Technology and the Workplace of the Future. *Academy of Management Executive, 13*(3), 17–29.
6	2	1997	Miles, R. E., Snow, C. S., Mathews, J. A., Miles, G., Coleman, H. J., Jr. (1997). Organizing in the Knowledge Age: Anticipating the Cellular Form. *Academy of Management Executive, 11*(4), 7–20.
5	2	1997	Cianni, M., & Wnuck, D. (1997). Individual Growth and Team Enhancement: Moving Toward a New Model of Career Development. *Academy of Management Executive, 11*(1), 105–115.
4	2	1996	Allred, B. B., Snow, C. C., Wiles, R. (1997). Characteristics of Managerial Careers in the 21st Century. *Academy of Management Executive, 10*(4), 17–27.
3	2	1996	Brousseau, K. R., Driver, M. J., Eneroth, K., & Larson, R. (1996). Career Pandemonium: Realigning Organizations and Individuals. *Academy of Management Executive, 10*(4), 52–66.
2	2	1995	Sadowski, S. T. (1995). Better Change: Best Practices for Transforming your Organization. *Academy of Management Executive, 9*(1), 91–93.
1	8	1992	Peterson, P. B. (1992). A Systems Approach to Quality Improvement. *Academy of Management Executive, 6*(4), 91–94.

Academy of Management Journal

Ref #	Class. Code	Year	Journal Articles
32	1	2007	Burt, R. S. (2007). Second Hand Brokerage: Evidence on the Importance of Local Structure for Managers, Bankers, and Analysts. *Academy of Management Journal, 50*(1), 119–148.
31	1	2005	King, A. A., Lenox, M. J., & Terlaak, A. (2005). The Strategic Use of Decentralized Institutions: Exploring Certifications with the ISO 14001 Management Standard. *Academy of Management Journal, 48*(6), 1091–1106.
30	2,4	2004	Kirkman, B. L. (2004). The Impact of Team Empowerment on Virtual Team Performance: The Moderating Role of Face-to-Face Interaction. *Academy of Management Journal, 47*(2), 175–192.
29	2	2003	Van Der Vegt, G. S., Van Der Vegt, E., & Oosterhof, A. (2003). Information Dissimilarity and Organizational Citizenship Behavior: The Role of Intra-Team Interdependence and Team Identification. *Academy of Management Journal, 46*(6), 715–727.
28	4	2003	Green, S. G., Welsh, M. A., & Dehler, G. E. (2003). Advocacy, Performance, and Threshold Influences on Decisions to Terminate New Product Development. *Academy of Management Journal, 46*(4), 419–434.

(continued next page)

27	1,2	2003	Bunderson, S. J. (2003). Team Member Functional Background and Involvement in Management Teams: Direct Effects and the Moderating Role of Power Centralization. *Academy of Management Journal, 46*(4), 458–474.
26	1	2002	Yakura, E. K. (2002). Charting Time: Timelines as Temporal Boundary Objects. *Academy of Management Journal, 45*(5), 956–970.
25	4,6	2002	Lewis, M. W., Welsh, A. M., Dehler, G. E., & Green, S. G. (2002). Product Development Tensions: Exploring Contrasting Styles of Project Management. *Academy of Management Journal, 45*(3), 546–564.
24	2	1998	Uhl-Bien, M., & Graen, G. B. (1998). Individual Self Management: Analysis of Professionals' Self-Managing Activities in Functional and Cross-Functional Work Teams. *Academy of Management Journal, 41*(3), 340–350.
23	2,4	1996	Dougherty, D., & Hardy, C. (1996). Sustained Product Innovation in Large, Mature Organizations: Overcoming Innovation-to-Organization Problems. *Academy of Management Journal, 39*(5), 1120–1153.
22	1,2	1996	Amabile, T. M., Conti, R., Coon, H., Lazenby, J., & Herron, M. (1996). Assessing the Work Environment of Creativity. *Academy of Management Journal, 39*(5), 1154–1184.
21	2	1996	Denison, D. R., Hart, S. L., & Kahn, J. A. (1996). From Chimneys to Cross-Functional Teams: Developing and Validating a Diagnostic Model. *Academy of Management Journal, 39*(4), 1005–1023.
20	7	1996	Miller, D., & Shamsie, J. (1996). The Resource-Based View of the Firm in Two Environments: The Hollywood Film Studios from 1936 to 1965. *Academy of Management Journal, 39*(3), 519–543.
19	4,6	1993	Leonard-Barton, D. (1993). Developer-User Interaction and User Satisfaction in Internal Technology Transfer. *Academy of Management Journal, 36*(5), 1125–1139.
18	1,2	1993	Harrison, P. D., & Harrell, A. (1993). Impact of "Adverse Selection" on Managers' Project Evaluation Decisions. *Academy of Management Journal, 36*(1), 635–642.
17	1	1993	Conlon, D. E., & Garland, H. (1993). The Role of Project Completion Information in Resource Allocation Decisions. *Academy of Management Journal, 36*(2), 402–413.
16	2,4	1988	Kazanjian, R. K. (1988). Relation of Dominant Problems to Stages Growth in Technology-Based New Ventures. *Academy of Management Journal, 31*(2), 257–279.
15	1,2	1986	Joyce, W. F. (1986). Matrix Organization: A Social Experiment. *Academy of Management Journal, 29*(3), 536–561.
14	6	1985	Katz, R., & Allen, T. J. (1985). Project Performance and the Locus of Influence in the R&D Matrix. *Academy of Management Journal, 28*(1), 67–87.

(continued next page)

13	2,6	1978	Dunne, E. J., Jr., Stahl, M. J., & Melhart, L. J., Jr. (1978). Influence Source of Project and Functional Managers in Matrix Organizations. *Academy of Management Journal*, *21*(1), 135–140.
12	6	1976	Cook, D. L., & Granger, J. C. (1976). Current Status of Project Management Instruction in American Colleges and Universities. *Academy of Management Journal*, *19*(2), 323–328.
11	6,7	1976	Pekar, P. P., Jr., & Burack, E. H. (1976). Management Control of Strategic Plans through Adaptive Techniques. *Academy of Management Journal*, *19*(1), 79–97.
10	1,6	1975	Fuller, J. A. (1975). A Linear Programming Approach to Aggregate Scheduling. *Academy of Management Journal*, *18*(1), 129–136.
9	1,2	1974	Thamhain, H. J., & Gemmil, G. R. (1974). Influence of Project Managers: Some Project Performance Correlates. *Academy of Management Journal*, *17*(2), 216–224.
8	2,6	1973	Hunt, R. G., & Rubin, I. S. (1973). Approaches to Managerial Control in Interpenetrating Systems: The Case of Government-Industry Relations. *Academy of Management Journal*, *16*(2), 296–311.
7	2,6	1973	Butler, A. G. (1973). Project Management: A Study of Organizational Conflict. *Academy of Management Journal*, *16*(1), 84–101.
6	1,6	1970	Wilemon, D. L. & Cicero, J. P. (1970). Project Manager: Anomalies and Ambiguities. *Academy of Management Journal*, *13*(3), 269–282.
5	1	1969	Paul, R. J. (1969). Communications. *Academy of Management Journal*, *12*(3), 383–384.
4	1,6	1968	Delionback, L. M., & Meinhart, W. A. (1968). Project Management: An Incentive Contracting Decision Model. *Academy of Management Journal*, *11*(4), 427–434.
3	2,6	1968	Hodgetts, R. M. (1968). Leadership Techniques in Project Organization. *Academy of Management Journal*, *11*(2), 211–219.
2	4,6	1967	Goodman, R. A. (1967). Ambiguous Authority Definition in Project Management. *Academy of Management Journal*, *10*(4), 13–18.
1	1	1964	Roman, D. D. (1964). Project Management Recognizes R&D Performance. *Academy of Management Journal*, *7*(1), 7–20.

Academy of Management Review

Ref #	Class. Code	Year	Journal Articles
11	1,2,6	2007	Gottschalg, O., & Zollo, M. (2007). Interest Alignment and Competitive Advantage. *Academy of Management Review, 32*(2), 418–437.
10	1,4,7	2004	Gerwin, D. (2004). Coordinating New Product Development in Strategic Alliances. *Academy of Management Review, 29*(2), 241–257.
9	1,7	2004	McGrath, R. G., Ferrier, W. J., & Mendelow, A. L. (2004). Real Options as Engines of Choice and Heterogeneity. *Academy of Management Review, 29*(1), 86–101.
8	2	2001	Waller, M. J., Conte, J. M., Gibson, C. B., & Carpenter, M. A.. (2001). The Effect of Individual Perceptions of Deadlines on Team Performance. *Academy of Management Review, 26*(4), 586–600.
7	1,2	1999	Drazin, R., Glynn, M. A., & Kazanjian, R. K. (1999). Multi-level Theorizing About Creativity in Organizations: A Sensemaking Perspective. *Academy of Management Review, 24*(2), 286.
6	2,4	1996	Kessler, E. H., & Chakrabarti, A. K. (1996). Innovation Speed: A Conceptual Model of Context, Antecedents, and Outcomes. *Academy of Management Review, 21*(4), 1143–1191.
5	1,6,7	1984	Northcraft, G. B., & Wolf, G. (1984). Dollars, Sense, and Sunk Costs: A Life Cycle Model of Resource Allocation Decisions. *Academy of Management Review, 9*(2), 225.
4	1,2,6	1983	Nuti, P. C. (1983). Implementation Approaches for Project Planning. *Academy of Management Review, 8*(4), 600.
3	1	1980	Bracker, J. (1980). The Historical Development of the Strategic Management Concept. *Academy of Management Review, 5*(2), 219.
2	1,6	1979	Kolodny, H. F. (1979). Evolution to a Matrix Organization. *Academy of Management Review, 4*(4), 543.
1	2,6	1978	Smith, H. R. (1978). A Socio-Biological Look at Matrix. *Academy of Management Review, 3*(4), 922.

Interfaces

Ref #	Class. Code	Year	Journal Articles
33	1,6	2007	Srinivasan, M. M, Best, W. D., & Chandrasekaran, S. (2007). Warner Robins Air Logistics Center Streamlines Aircraft Repair and Overhaul. *Interfaces, 37*(1), 7–21.
32	6,8	2006	Ferratt, T. W., Ahire, S., & De, P. (2006). Achieving Success in Large Projects; Implications from a Study of ERP Implementations. *Interfaces, 36*(5), 458–469.

(continued next page)

31	1,6	2006	Woosley, G. (2006). The Fifth Column: Homage to Doc Savage 2, or "Yes I know You Can Solve It with an Optimum Method, but What Are You Going to Tell Your Customer If He Asks, 'How Does He Do That?'" *Interfaces, 36*(4), 342–343.
30	1	2004	Flowers, D. (2004). ASP, The Art and Science of Practice: Getting the R in Contact. *Interfaces, 34*(5), 377–382.
29	1,6	2001	Ahire, S. L. (2001). Linking Operations Management Students Directly to the Real World. *Interfaces, 31*(5), 104–120.
28	1,6	2000	Portougal, V., & Robb, D. J. (2000). Production Scheduling Theory: Just Where Is It Applicable? *Interfaces, 37*(1), 64–76.
27	1,6,7	2000	LeBlanc, L. J., Randels, D., Jr., & Swann, T. K. (2000). Heery International's Spreadsheet Optimization Model for Assigning Managers to Construction Projects. *Interfaces, 30*(30), 95–106.
26	1	2000	Fildes, R., & Ranyard, J. (2000). Internal OR Consulting: Effective Practice in a Changing Environment. *Interfaces, 30*(5), 34–50.
25	3,6,8	1999	Kolisch, R. (1999). Resource Allocation Capabilities of Commercial Project Management Software Packages. *Interfaces, 29*(4), 19–31.
24	1,6	1998	Murphy, F. H. (1998). The Occasional Observer: Some Simple Precepts for Project Success. *Interfaces, 28*(5), 24–28.
23	6	1995	Orman, A. (1995). Project Management: Planning and Control, Second Edition. *Interfaces, 25*(3), 114–115.
22	2,4,6	1993	Burnett, W. M., Monetta, D. J., & Silverman, B. G. (1993). How the Gas Research Institute (GRI) Helped Transform the US Natural Gas Industry. *Interfaces, 23*(1), 44–58.
21	1,6	1990	Trippi, R. R. (1990) Decision Support and Expert Systems for Real Estate Investment Decisions: A Review. *Interfaces, 20*(5), 50–60.
20	1,4	1990	Gass, S. I. (1990). Model World: Have Model, Will Travel. *Interfaces, 20*(2), 67–71.
19	4,6	1989	Machol, R. E. (1989). Misapplications Reviews: Strange Postures. *Interfaces, 19*(6), 62–66.
18	3,6	1988	Wasil, E.A., & Assad, A. A. (1988). Project Management on the PC: Software, Applications, and Trends. *Interfaces, 18*(2), 75–84.
17	2,6	1987	Schultz, R. L., Slevin, D. P., & Pinto, J. K. (1987). Strategy and Tactics in a Process Model of Project Implementation. *Interfaces, 17*(3), 34–46.
16	1,6	1985	Cropper, S., & Bennet, P. (1985). Testing Times: Dilemmas in an Action Research Project. *Interfaces, 15*(5), 71–80.
15	1	1984	Harrison, T. P., & de Kluyver, C. A. (1984). MS/OR and the Forest Products Industry: New Directions. *Interfaces, 14*(5), 1–7.

(continued next page)

14	1,3,6	1982	Vazsonyi, A. (1982). Computer-Supported Gedanken Experiments. *Interfaces, 12*(4), 34–41.
13	1,6	1982	Hoffman, G. M. (1982). Project Cost Control: Dynamic Risk Analysis of Randomly Ordered Sequential Decisions Under Uncertainty. *Interfaces, 12*(3), 45–51.
12	1	1981	Schonberger, R. (Oct 1981). Why Projects Are "Always" Late: A Rationale Based on Manual Simulation of A PERT/CPM Network. *Interfaces, 11*(5), 66–70.
11	1	1981	Maxfield, M. W. (1981). Sequencing and Scheduling in Real Time—Quickly. *Interfaces, 11*(3), 40–43.
10	1,6	1981	Souder, W. E. (1981). Project Management—A Systems Approach to Planning, Scheduling and Controlling. *Interfaces, 11*(3), 92–93.
9	2	1981	Woosley, G. (1981). Yet Another Essay on Effective Communication or on Learning Where to Begin, How to Listen, and When to Stop. *Interfaces, 11*(1), 10–12.
8	1,6	1980	Luken, T. P., Otten, A., & Haugen, P. S. (1980). Quick and Clean: An Aspect of the IE/OR Interface. *Interfaces, 10*(5), 1–6.
7	1,2,6	1980	Graham, R. J. (1980). On the Death of Theory Y. *Interfaces, 10*(5), 76–79.
6	1,6	1975	Reisman, A. (1975). The By-Line Dilemma. *Interfaces, 5*(3), 36–37.
5	1,7	1974	Shycon, H. N. (1974). Perspectives on MS Applications. *Interfaces, 4*(3), 23–25.
4	1,4,8	1974	Bucatinski, J. (1974). Using PERT to Manage High Technology Projects. *Interfaces, 4*(3), 84–89.
3	1,6	1973	Thomas, E. D., & Coveleski, D. P. (1973). Planning Nuclear Equipment Manufacturing. *Interfaces, 3*(3), 18–29.
2	1,6	1972	Bucatinsky, J., & Cutler, R. S. (1972). SOAP: A Management Science Success Story. *Interfaces, 3*(1), 52–54.
1	1,2,6	1972	Shycon, H. N. (1972). All Around the Model: Perspectives on MS Applications. *Interfaces, 2*(4), 45–48.

Operations Research

Ref #	Class. Code	Year	Journal Articles
26	1,4,6	2005	Gustafsson, J., & Salo, A. (2005). Contingent Portfolio Programming for the Management of Risky Projects. *Operations Research, 53*(6), 946–956.
25	1,3	2003	Dillon, R. L., Paté-Cornell, E. M., & Guikema, S. D. (2003). Programmatic Risk Analysis for Critical Engineering Systems Under Tight Resource Constraints. *Operations Research, 51*(3), 354.
24	1,5	2000	Gutierrez, G. & Paul, A. (2000). Analysis of the Effects of Uncertainty, Risk-Pooling, and Subcontracting Mechanisms on Project Performance. *Operations Research, 48*(6), 927, 12.

(continued next page)

23	1,6,7	1999	Blocher, J. D., Chand, S., & Sengupta, K. (1999). The Changeover Scheduling Problem with Time and Cost Considerations: Analytical Results and a Forward Algorithm. *Operations Research, 47*(4), 559–569.
22	1	1998	Smith, J. E., & McCardle, K. F. (1998). Valuing Oil Properties: Integrating Option Pricing and Decision Analysis Approaches. *Operations Research, 46*(2), 198–217.
21	1,6	1997	Demeulemeester, E. L., & Herroelen, W. S. (1997). A Branch-and-Bound Procedure for the Generalized Resource-Constrained Project Scheduling Problem. *Operations Research, 45*(2), 201–212.
20	1,6	1997	De, P., Dunne, J. E., Ghosh, J. B., & Wells, C. E. (1997). Complexity of the Discrete Time-Cost Tradeoff Problem for Project Networks. *Operations Research, 45*(2), 302–306.
19	1,6	1997	Buss, A. H., & Rosenblatt, M. J. (1997). Activity Delay in Stochastic Project Networks. *Operations Research, 45*(1), 126–139.
18	6,7,8	1995	Birge, J. R., & Maddox, M. J. (1995). Bounds on Expected Project Tardiness. *Operations Research, 43*(5), 838–850.
17	1,6	1993	Adler, L., Fraiman, N., Kobacker, E., Pinedo, M., Plotnicoff, J. C., & Wu, I. P. (1993). BPSS: A Scheduling Support System for the Packaging Industry. *Operations Research, 41*(4), 641–648.
16	5,6	1992	Henig, M. I., & Levin, N. (1992). Joint Production Planning and Product Delivery Commitments with Random Yield. *Operations Research, 40*(2), 404–409.
15	1,5,6	1990	Dada, M., & Srikanth, K. N. (1990). Monopolistic Pricing and the Learning Curve: An Algorithmic Approach. *Operations Research, 38*(4), 656–666.
14	1,6	1990	Brown, G. G., Goodman, C. E., & Wood, K. R. (1990). Annual Scheduling of Atlantic Fleet Naval Combatants. *Operations Research, 38*(2), 249–260.
13	1,3,6	1987	Van Roy, T. J., & Wolsey, L. A. (1987). Solving Mixed Integer Programming Problems Using Automatic Reformation. Operations Research, 35(1), 45–57.
12	1,5,6	1986	Axaster, S. (1986). On The Feasibility Of Aggregate Production Plans. *Operations Research, 34*(5), 796–800.
11	1,3,6	1981	Moeller, G. L., & Digman, L. A. (1981). Operations Planning with VERT. *Operations Research, 29*(4), 676–697.
10	1	1977	Robillard P., & Trahan, M. (1977). The Completion Time of PERT Networks. Operations Research, 25(1), 15–29.
9	1	1976	Dyer, J. S., & Miles, R. F. (1976). An Actual Application of Collective Choice Theory to the Selection of Trajectories for the Mariner Jupiter/Saturn. Operations Research, 24(2), 220–245.
8	1,5,6	1975	Kleindorfer, P. R., & Newson, E. F. P. (1975). A Lower Bounding Structure for Lot-Size Scheduling Problems. *Operations Research, 23*(2), 299–312.

(continued next page)

7	1,6	1972	Kabak, I. W. (1972). On Scheduling the Delivery of Babies. *Operations Research, 20*(1), 19–23.
6	1,8	1970	Schrage, L. (1970). Solving Resource-Constrained Network Problems by Implicit Enumeration—Nonpreemptive Case. Operations Research, 18(2), 263–278.
5	1,3,6	1970	Schussel, G., & Price, S. (1970). A Case History in Optimum Inventory Scheduling. *Operations Research, 18*(1), 1–23.
4	1,6	1967	Crowston, W., & Thompson, G. L. (1967). Decision CPM: A Method for Simultaneous Planning, Scheduling, and Control of Projects. *Operations Research, 15*(3), 407–426.
3	1,5,7	1966	Zangill, W.I. (1966). A Deterministic Multiproduct, Multifacility Production and Inventory Model. *Operations Research, 14*(3), 486–507.
2	1,6,8	1965	Martin, J. J. (1965). Distribution of the Time Through a Directed, Acyclic Network. *Operations Research, 13*(1), 46–66.
1	1,5	1957	Morris, W. T. (1957). Education In Operations Research at the Ohio State University. Operations Research, 5(6), 861–862.

Management Science

Ref #	Class. Code	Year	Journal Articles
91	6,7	2007	Pacheco-de-Almeida, G. & Zemesky, P. (2007). The Timing of Resource Development and Sustainable Competitive Advantage. *Management Science, 53*(4), 651–666.
90	1,4,6	2007	Mitchell, V. L., & Nault, B. R. (2007). Cooperative Planning, Uncertainty, and Managerial Control in Concurrent Design. *Management Science, 53*(3), 375–389.
89	1,6	2006	Vereecke, A., Van Dierdonck, R., & De Meyer, A. (2006). A Typology of Plants in Global Manufacturing Networks. *Management Science, 52*(11), 1737–1750.
88	1,2,6	2006	Haas, M. R. (2006). Knowledge Gathering, Team Capabilities, and Project Performance in Challenging Work Environments. *Management Science, 52*(8), 1170–1184.
87	3,4	2006	Grewal, R., Lilien, G. L., Mallapragada, G. (2006). Location, Location, Location: How Network Embeddedness Affects Project Success in Open Source Systems. *Management Science, 52*(7), 1043–1046.
86	3,6	2006	Baldwin, C. Y., & Clark, K. B. (2006). The Architecture of Participation: Does Code Architecture Mitigate Free Riding in the Open Source Development Model? *Management Science, 52*(7), 1116–1127.
85	1,6	2006	Trout, M. J., Pang, W.-K., Hou, S.-H. (2006). Behavioral Estimation of Mathematical Programming Objective Function Coefficients. *Management Science, 52*(3), 422–434.
84	3,6,7	2005	Santiago, L. P., & Vakili, P. (2005). On the Value of Flexibility in R&D Projects. *Management Science, 51*(8), 1206–1218.

(continued next page)

83	1,6,7	2005	Szmerekovsky, J. G. (2005). The Impact of Contractor Behavior on the Client's Payment-Scheduling Problem. *Management Science, 51*(4), 629–640.
82	2,6	2004	Sommer, S. C., & Loch, C. H. (2004). Selectionism and Learning in Projects with Complexity and Unforeseeable Uncertainty. *Management Science, 50*(10), 1334–1347.
81	4	2004	Bajaj, A., Kekre, S., & Srinivasan, K.(2004). Managing NPD: Cost and Schedule Performance in Design and Manufacturing. *Management Science, 50*(4), 527–536.
80	3,5,6	2003	Sivaramakrishnan, K., & Gopal, A. (2003). Contracts in Off-shore Development. *Management Science, 49*(12), 1671–1683.
79	1,6	2003	Ahuja, R. K., Hochbaum, D. S., & Orlin, J. B. (2003). Solving the Convex Cost Integer Dual Network Flow Problem. *Management Science 49*(7), 950–964.
78	1,6	2003	Vairaktarakis, G. L. (2003). The Value of Resource Flexibility in the Resource-Constrained Job Assignment Problem. *Management Science, 49*(6), 718–732.
77	1,2,6	2003	Mihm, J., Loch, C., & Huchzermeier, A. (2003). Problem-Solving Oscillations in Complex Engineering Projects. *Management Science, 49*(6), 733–750.
76	3,6	2003	Dye, R. A., & Sridhar, S. S. (2003). Investment Implications of Information Acquisition and Leakage. *Management Science, 49*(6), 767–783.
75	1,3	2003	Möhring, R. H., Schulz, A. S., Stork, F., & Uetz, M. (2003). Solving Project Scheduling Problems by Minimum Cut Computations. *Management Science, 49*(3), 330–350.
74	6	2002	Pich, M. T., Loch, C. H., & De Meyer, A. (2002). On Uncertainty, Ambiguity, and Complexity in Project Management. *Management Science, 48*(8), 1008–1023.
73	1,6	2002	Arya, A., Glover, J., & Routledge, B. R.. (2002). Project Assignment Rights and Incentives for Eliciting Ideas. *Management Science, 48*(7), 886–899.
72	1,6,7	2001	Vanhoucke, M., & Demeulemeester, E. (2001). On Maximizing the Net Present Value of a Project Under Renewable Resource Constraints. *Management Science, 47*(8), 1113–1121.
71	1,5,6	2001	Butler, J., Morrice, D. J., & Mullarkey, P. W. (2001). A Multiple Attribute Utility Theory Approach to Ranking and Selection. *Management Science, 47*(6), 800–816.
70	4,5,6	2001	Shenhar, A. J. (2001). One Size Does Not Fit All Projects: Exploring Classical Contingency Domains. *Management Science, 47*(3), 394–414.
69	1,4	2001	Krishnan, V., & Ulrich, K. T. (2001). Product Development Decisions: A Review of the Literature. Management Science, *47*(1), 1–21.
68	4,6	2001	Huchzermeier, A., & Loch, C. H. (2001). Project Management Under Risk: Using the Real Options Approach to Evaluate Flexibility in R&D. *Management Science, 47*(1), 85–101.

(continued next page)

67	4,7	2001	Tatikonda, M. V., & Montoya-Weiss, M. M. (2001). Integrating Operations and Marketing Perspectives of Product Innovation: The Influence of Organizational Process Factors and Capabilities on Development Performance. *Management Science, 47*(1), 151–172.
66	1,6	2000	Dorndorf, U., Pesch, E., & Phan-Huy, T. (2000). A Time-Oriented Branch-and-Bound Algorithm for Resource-Constrained Project Scheduling with Generalised Precedence Constraints. *Management Science, 46*(10), 1365–1384.
65	3,7	2000	Arya, A., Fellingham, J., Glover, J., & Sivaramakrishnan, K. (2000). Capital Budgeting, the Hold-Up Problem, and Information System Design. *Management Science, 46*(2), 205–216.
64	1,2,3	1999	Levitt, R. E., Thomsen, J., Christiansen, T. R., Kunz, J. C., Jin, Y., & Nass, C. (1999). Simulating Project Work Processes and Organizations: Toward a Micro-Contingency Theory of Organizational Design. *Management Science, 45*(11), 1479–1495.
63	3,6	1999	Maxwell, K., Van Wassenhove, L., & Dutta, S. (1999). Performance Evaluation of General and Company Specific Models in Software Development Effort Estimation. *Management Science, 45*(6), 787–803.
62	1,4,5	1999	Terwiesch, C., & Loch, C. H. (1999). Measuring the Effectiveness of Overlapping Development Activities. *Management Science, 45*(4), 455–465.
61	1,2,6	1999	Böttcher, J., Drexl, A., Kolisch, R., & Salewski, F. (1999). Project Scheduling Under Partially Renewable Resource Constraints. *Management Science, 45*(4), 543–559.
60	1,6	1999	Sprecher, A., & Drexl, A. (1999). Note: On Semi-Active Timetabling in Resource-Constrained Project Scheduling. *Management Science, 45*(3), 452–454.
59	3,7	1997	Banker, R. D., & Slaughter, S. A. (1997). A Field Study of Scale Economies in Software Maintenance. *Management Science, 43*(12), 1709–1725.
58	1,6	1997	Sox, C. R., Thomas, J. L., & McClain, J. O. (1997). Coordinating Production and Inventory to Improve Service. *Management Science, 43*(9), 1189–1197.
57	3,6	1996	Moenaert, R. K., & Souder, W. E. (1996). Context and Antecedents of Information Utility at the R&D/Marketing Interface. *Management Science, 42*(11), 1592–1610.
56	1,2,6	1993	Pinto, M. B., Pinto, J. K., & Prescott, J. E. (1993). Antecedents and Consequences of Project Team Cross-Functional Cooperation. *Management Science, 39*(10), 1281–1297.
55	1,3,6	1992	Demeulemeester, E., & Herroelen, W. (1992). A Branch-and-Bound Procedure for the Multiple Resource-Constrained Project Scheduling Problem. *Management Science, 38*(12), 1803–1818.
54	3,6	1992	Henderson, J. C., & Soonchul, L. (1992). Managing I/S Design Teams: A Control Theories Perspective. *Management Science, 38*(6), 757–777.

(continued next page)

53	1,6	1992	Drexl, A. (1991). Scheduling of Project Networks by Job Assignment. *Management Science, 37*(12), 1590–1602.
52	1,6	1991	Kamrad, B., & Ritchken, P. (1991). Multinomial Approximating Models for Options With k State Variables. *Management Science, 37*(12), 1640–1652.
51	6,7	1991	Carraway, R. L. & Schmidt, R. L. (1991). Notes: An Improved Discrete Dynamic Programming Algorithm for Allocating Resources Among Interdependent Projects. *Management Science, 37*(9), 1195–1200.
50	1,6	1991	Gutierrez, G. & Kouvelis, P. (1991). Parkinson's Law and Its Implications for Project Management. *Management Science, 37*(8), 990–1001.
49	2,5	1991	Oral, M., Kettani, O., & Lang, P. (1991). A Methodology for Collective Evaluation and Selection of Industrial R&D Projects. *Management Science, 37*(7), 871–885.
48	3,6	1989	Bell, C. E. (1989). Maintaining Project Networks in Automated Artificial Intelligence Planning. Management Science, 35(10), 1192–1214.
47	1,6	1989	Dewald, L. S., Lewis, P. A. W., & McKenzie, E. (1989). A Bivariate First-Order Autoregressive Time Series Model in Exponential Variables. *Management Science, 35*(10), 1236–1246.
46	4,5,6	1989	Clark, K. B. (1989). Project Scope and Project Performance: The Effect of Parts Strategy and Supplier Involvement on Product Development. *Management Science, 35*(10), 1247–1263.
45	1,6	1989	Mazzola, J. (1989). Generalized Assignment with Nonlinear Capacity Interaction. Management Science, 35(8), 923–941.
44	1,6	1988	Dumond, J., & Mabert, V. A. (1988). Evaluating Project Scheduling and Due Date Assignment Procedures: An Experimental Analysis. *Management Science, 34*(1), 101–118.
43	6,7	1986	Russell, R. A. (1986). A Comparison of Heurisitics for Scheduling Projects with Cash Flows and Resource Restrictions. *Management Science, 32*(10), 1291–1300.
42	6,7	1984	Patterson, J. H. (1984). A Comparison of Exact Approaches for Solving the Multiple Constrained Resource, Project Scheduling Problem. *Management Science, 30*(7), 854–867.
41	4,6	1984	Fox, E. G., Baker, N. R., & Bryant, J. L. (1984). Economics Models for R and D Project Selection in the Presence of Project Interactions. *Management Science, 30*(7), 890–902.
40	4,6	1983	Hetzner, W., Tornatzky, L. G., & Klein, K. J. (1983). Manufacturing Technology in the 1980's: A Survey of Federal Programs and Practices. *Management Science, 29*(8), 951–961.
39	1,4,6	1983	Libertore, M. J. & Titus, G. J. (1983). The Practice of Management Science in R&D Project Management. *Management Science, 29*(8), 962–974.
38	1,6	1983	Wlodzimierz, S., & Posner, M. E. (1983). A Transportation Type Aggregate Production Model with Backordering. *Management Science, 29*(2), 188–199.

(continued next page)

37	1,4,6	1983	Silverman, B. G. (1983). Project Appraisal Methodology: Market Penetration Elements. *Management Science, 29*(2), 210–224.
36	6,7	1982	Talbot, B. F. (1982). Resource-Constrained Project Scheduling with Time-Resource Tradeoffs: The Non-preemptive Case. *Management Science, 28*(10), 1197–1210.
35	1,3,6	1982	Graves, S. C. (1982). Using Langrangean Techniques to Solve Hierarchical Production Planning Problems. *Management Science, 28*(3), 260–275.
34	1,6	1982	Kurtulus, I., & Davis, E. W. (1982). Multi-Project Scheduling: Categorization of Heuristic Rules Performance. *Management Science, 28*(2), 161–172.
33	1,6	1981	Gupta, R. M., & Deisenroth, M. P. (1981). Comments on The Complexity Rating Factor for Layout Problems. *Management Science, 27*(12), 1460–1464.
32	1,6	1981	Węglarz, J. (1981). Project Scheduling with Continuously Divisible, Doubly Constrained Resources. *Management Science, 27*(9), 1040–1053.
31	1,4,6	1981	Kalymon, B. A. (1981). Methods of Large Project Assessment Given Uncertainty in Future Energy Pricing. *Management Science, 27*(4), 377–395.
30	1,6	1979	Hollway, C. A., Nelson, R. T., & Suraphongschai, V. (1979). Comparison of a Multi-Pass Heuristic Decomposition Procedure with Other Resource-Constrained Project Scheduling Procedures. *Management Science, 25*(9), 862–872.
29	1,6,7	1979	Anderson, J. & Narasimhan, R. (1979). Assessing Project Implementation Risk: A Methodological Approach. *Management Science, 25*(6), 512–521.
28	1,4,6	1979	Birnbaum, P. H. (1979). A Theory of Academic Inter-disciplinary Research Performance: A Contingency and Path Analysis Approach. *Management Science, 25*(3), 231–242.
27	1,6	1979	Graves, S. C. (1979). On the Deterministic Demand Multi-Product Single-Machine Lot Scheduling Problem. *Management Science, 25*(3), 276–280.
26	2,4	1978	Dailey, R. C. (1978). The Role of Team and Task Characteristics in R&D Team Collaborative Problem Solving and Productivity. *Management Science, 24*(15), 1579–1588.
25	6,7	1977	Dessouky, M. I., & Philips, S., Jr. (1977). Solving The Project Time/Cost Tradeoff Problem Using the Minimal Cut Concept. *Management Science, 24*(4), 393–400.
24	1,6,7	1977	Burt, J. M. (1977). Planning and Dynamic Control of Projects Under Uncertainty. *Management Science, 24*(3), 249–258.
23	1,2,6	1977	Thomas, J., & McClain, J. O. (1977). Horizon Effects in Aggregate Production Planning with Seasonal Demand. *Management Science, 23*(7), 728–736.
22	1,3,6	1975	Robinson, D. R. (1975). A Dynamic Programming Solution to Cost-Time Tradeoff for CPM. *Management Science, 22*(2), 158–166.

(continued next page)

21	1,6,7	1975	Goyal, S. K. (1975). A Note on "A Simple CPM Time-Cost Tradeoff Algorithm." *Management Science, 21*(6), 718–722.
20	1,3,6	1975	Ratliff, D. H., Sicilia, T. G., & Lubore, S. H. (1975). Finding the n Most Vital Links in Flow Networks. *Management Science, 21*(5), 531–539.
19	1,6	1975	Schrage, L. (1975). Minimizing the Time-in-System Variance for a Finite Jobset. *Management Science, 21*(5), 540–543.
18	3,6,7	1974	Blackburn, J. D., & Kunreuther, H. (1974). Planning Horizons for the Dynamic Lot Size Model with Backlogging. *Management Science, 21*(3), 251–255.
17	1,6	1974	Leitch, R. A. (1974). Marketing Strategy and the Optimal Production Schedule. Management Science, *21*(3), 302–312.
16	1,6	1974	Maher, P. M., & Rubenstein, A. H. (1974). Factors Affecting Adoption of a Quantitative Method for R&D Project Selection. *Management Science, 21*(2), 119–129.
15	1,6	1974	Patterson, J. H., & Huber, W. D. (1974). A Horizon-Varying, Zero-One Approach to Project Scheduling. *Management Science, 20*(6), 990–998.
14	1,5,6	1972	Thomas, J. E., Manton, E. J., & Stoms, J. M. (1972). An Operations Research Approach to the Management of Government Cost-Plus-Award-Fee Contracts. Management Science, *18*(6), B358–B359.
13	1	1971	Moore, J. R., Jr. (1971). Forecasting and Scheduling for Past-Model Replacement Parts. *Management Science, 18*(4), B200–B213.
12	1,2	1971	Ansoff, H. I. & Brandenburg, R. G. (1971). A Language for Organization Design: Part I. *Management Science, 17*(12), B705–B716
11	1,6,7	1971	Siemens, N. (1971). A Simple CPM Time-Cost Tradeoff Algorithm. *Management Science, 17*(6), B354–B363.
10	4	1969	Abernathy, W. J., & Rosenbloom, R. S. (1969). Parallel Strategies in Development Projects. Management Science, *15*(10), B486–B505.
9	1,6	1969	Kunreuther, H. (1969). Extension of Bowman's Theory on Managerial Decision-Making. Management Science, *15*(8), B415–B439.
8	1,2	1968	Rath, G. J. (1968). Management Science in University Operation. Management Science, *14*(6), B373–B384.
7	1,2	1968	Dean, B. V. (1968). Critique of: "Management Science in University Operation." Management Science, *14*(6), B385–B387.
6	1	1967	Jones, C. H. (1967). Parametric Production Planning. Management Science, *13*(11), 843–866.
5	1,6,7	1965	Blanning, R. W., Rao, A. G, & Rothkopf, M. H. (1965). Communications to the Editor. *Management Science,* 12(1), 145–149.
4	1,3	1964	Bhende, V. P. (1964). Development Planning in Under-Developed Countries. Management Science, *10*(4), 796–809.

(continued next page)

3	1,3	1961	Klein, M. (1961). On Production Smoothing. Management Science, 7(3), 286–293.
2	3,6,7	1958	Rogers, J. (1958). A Computational Approach to the Economic Lot Scheduling Problem. *Management Science*, 4(3), 264–291.
1	1,3	1957	Charnes, A., & Cooper, W. W. (1957). Management Models and Industrial Applications of Linear Programming. Management Science, 4(1), 38–91.

Organization Science

Ref #	Class. Code	Year	Journal Articles
5	1,2,4	2007	Li, H., Bingham, J. B., & Umphress, E. E. (2007). Fairness from the Top: Perceived Procedural Justice and Collaborative Problem Solving in New Product Development. *Organization Science, 18(2)*, 200–216.
4	2,4,6	2004	Gerwin, D., & Ferris, J. S. (2004). Organizing New Product Development Projects in Strategic Alliances. Organization Science, 15(1), 22–37.
3	2,6	2003	Pitsis, T., Clegg, S. R., Marosszeky, M., & Rura-Polley, T. (2003). Constructing the Olympic Dream: A Future Perfect Strategy of Project Management. *Organization Science, 14(5)*, 574–590.
2	2,6	2003	O'Connor, G. C., Rice, M. P., Peters, L., & Veryzer, R. W. (2003). Managing Interdisciplinary, Longitudinal Research Teams: Extending Grounded Theory-Building Methodologies. *Organization Science, 14(4)*, 353–373.
1	1,2,3	1996	Kirsch, L. J. (1996). The Management of Complex Tasks in Organizations: Controlling the Systems Development Process. *Organization Science, 7(1)*, 1–21.

Information Systems Research

Ref #	Class. Code	Year	Journal Articles
17	3	2006	Stewart, K. J., Ammeter, A. P., & Maruping, L. M. (2006). Impacts of License Choice and Organizational Sponsorship on User Interest and Development Activity in Open Software Projects. Information Systems Research, 17(2), 126–144.
16	3,7	2006	Ranganathan, C., & Brown, C. V. (2006). ERP Investments and the Market Value of Firms: Toward an Understanding of Influential ERP Project Variables. *Information Systems Research, 17(2)*, 145–161.
15	3	2005	Levina, N. (2005). Collaborating on Multiparty Information Systems Development Projects: A Collective Reflection-in-Action View. *Information Systems Research, 16(2)*, 109–130.

(continued next page)

14	3	2004	Kirsch, L. J. (2004). Deploying Common Systems Globally: The Dynamics of Control. *Information Systems Research, 15*(4), 374–395.
13	3, 4	2004	Krishnan, M. S., Mukhopadhyay, T., & Kriebel, C. H. (2004). A Decision Model for Software Maintenance. *Information Systems Research, 15*(4), 396–412.
12	3,7	2004	Fichman, R. G. (2004). Real Options and IT Platform Adoption: Implications for Theory and Practice. *Information Systems Research, 15*(2), 132–154.
11	3	2004	Chiang, R. I., & Mookerjee, V. S. (2004). A Fault Threshold Policy to Manage Software Development Projects. *Information Systems Research, 15*(1), 3–21.
10	3	2003	Choudhury, V., & Sabherwal, R. (2003). Portfolios of Control in Outsourced Software Development Projects. *Information Systems Research, 14*(3), 291–314.
9	1,3,4	2002	Wheeler, B. C. (2002). NEBIC: A Dynamic Capabilities Theory for Assessing Net-Enablement. *Information Systems Research, 13*(2), 125–146.
8	3,7	2000	Banker, R. D., & Slaughter, S. A. (2000). The Moderating Effects of Structure on Volatility and Complexity in Software Enhancement. *Information Systems Research, 11*(3), 219.
7	3,8	1998	Lyytinen, K., & Mathiassen, L. (1998). Attention Shaping and Software Risk—A Categorical Analysis of Four Classical Risk Management Approaches. *Information Systems Research, 9*(3), 233–255.
6	3,4,7	1998	Guinan, P. J., Cooprider, J. G., & Faraj, S. (1998). Enabling Software Development Team Performance During Requirements Definition: A Behavioral Versus Technical Approach. *Information Systems Research, 9*(2), 101–125.
5	1,2,3	1997	Kirsch, L. J. (1997). Portfolios of Control Modes and IS Project Management. *Information Systems Research, 8*(3), 215.
4	3	1995	Nidumolu, S. (1995). The Effect of Coordination and Uncertainty on Software Project Performance: Residual Performance Risk as an Intervening Variable. *Information Systems Research, 6*(3), 191–219.
3	2,3,5	1992	Banker. R. D., & Kemerer, C. F. (1992). Performance Evaluation Metrics for Information Systems Development: A Principal-Agent Model. *Information Systems Research, 3*(4), 379–400.
2	2,3,6	1991	Vicinanza, S. S., Mukhopadhyay, T., Prietula, M. J. (1991). Software-Effort Estimation: An Exploratory Study of Expert Performance. Information Systems Research, 2(4), 243–262.
1	1,3,7	1991	Jain, H. K., Tanniru, M. R., & Fazlollahi, B. (1991). MCDM Approach for Generating and Evaluating Alternatives in Requirement Analysis. *Information Systems Research, 2*(3), 223–239.

Ref #	Class. Code	Year	Journal Articles
48	6,7	2005	Sirkin, H. L, Keenan, P., & Jackson, A. (2005) The Hard Side of Change Management. *Harvard Business Review, 83*(10), 108–118.
47	2,7	2005	Thurm, D. (2005). Master of the House. *Harvard Business Review, 83*(10), 120–129.
46	6	2005	Mankins, M. C., & Steele, R. (2005). Turning Great Strategy Into Great Performance. *Harvard Business Review, 83*(7/8), 64–72.
45	2,6	2005	Fischer, B., & Boynton, A. (2005). Virtuoso Teams. *Harvard Business Review, 83*(7/8), 116–123.
44	6	2004	MacCormack, A. (2004). Management Lessons from Mars. *Harvard Business Review, 82*(5), 18–19.
43	7	2003	Fleming, Q. W., & Koppelman, J. M. (2003). What's Your Project's Real Price Tag. *Harvard Business Review, 81*(9), 20–22.
42	2,6	2003	Matta, N. E., & Ashkenas, R. N. (2003). Why Good Projects Fail Anyway. *Harvard Business Review, 82*(9), 109–114.
41	1	2002	Wolpert, J. D. (2002). Breaking Out of the Innovation Box. *Harvard Business Review, 80*(8), 76–83.
40	7	2001	Engwall, M., & Svensson, C. (2001). Cheetah Teams. *Harvard Business Review, 79*(2), 20–21.
39	1	2001	Epplinger, S. D. (2001). Innovation at the Speed of information. *Harvard Business Review, 79*(1), 149–158.
38	6	1998	Elton, J., & Roe, J. (1998). Bringing Discipline to Project Management. *Harvard Business Review, 76*(2), 153–159.
37	8	1996	Adler, S., Nguyen, A. M, & Schwerer, E. (1996). Getting the Most Out of Your Product Development Process. *Harvard Business Review, 74*(2), 134–152.
36	7	1995	Dixit, A. K., & Pindyck, R. S. (1995). The Options Approach to Capital Investment. *Harvard Business Review, 73*(3), 105–115.
35	2,6	1994	Hamel, G., & Prahalad, C. K. (1994). Competing for the Future. *Harvard Business Review, 72*(4), 122.
34	2,6	1993	Hall, G., Rosenthal, J., Wade, J. (1993). How To Make Reengineering Really Work. *Harvard Business Review, 71*(6), 119–131.
33	1	1993	Iansiti, M. (1993). Real World R&D: Jumping the Product Generation Gap. *Harvard Business Review, 71*(3), 138–147.
32	1,6	1992	Wheelwright, S. C., & Clark, K. B. (1992). Creating Project Plans to Focus Product Development. *Harvard Business Review, 70*(2), 67–83.
31	5	1989	Macomber, J. D. (1989). You Can Manage Construction Risks. *Harvard Business Review, 67*(2), 155–165.
30	5	1989	Spiegelman, K. A. (1989). Choosing an Architect. *Harvard Business Review, 67*(2), 162.

(continued next page)

29	6	1987	Gulliver, F. R. (1987). Post-Project Appraisal. *Harvard Business Review, 65*(2), 128–132.
28	1,6	1986	Lee, T. H., Fisher, J. C., & Yau, T. S. (1986). Is Your R&D on Track? *Harvard Business Review, 64*(1), 34–44.
27	1,6	1986	Takeuchi, H., & Ikujiro, N. (1986). The New Product Development Game. *Harvard Business Review, 64*(1), 137–146.
26	2	1985	Clawson, R. T. (1985). Controlling the Manufacturing Start-Up. *Harvard Business Review, 63*(3), 6–20.
25	6	1985	Davis, D. (1985). New Projects: Beware of False Economies. *Harvard Business Review, 63*(2), 95–101.
24	2,8	1984	McDonough, E. F., III. (1984). Quick-Response New Product Development. *Harvard Business Review, 62*(5), 52–54.
23	2,6	1984	Hurst, D. K. (1984). Of Boxes, Bubbles, and Effective Management. *Harvard Business Review, 62*(3), 78–88.
22	6	1984	Lambrix, R. J., & Singhvi, S. S. (1984). Pre-Approval Audits of Capital Projects. *Harvard Business Review, 62*(2), 12–14.
21	1	1982	Rosenbloom, R. S. & Kantrow, A. M. (1982). The Nurturing of Corporate Research. *Harvard Business Review, 60*(1), 115–123.
20	3	1981	McFarlan, F. W. (1981). Portfolio Approach to Information Systems. *Harvard Business Review, 59*(5), 142–150.
19	2	1975	Gluck, F. W., & Foster, R. N. (1975). Managing Technological Change: A Box of Cigars for Brad. *Harvard Business Review, 53*(5), 139–150.
18	2	1974	Culliton, J. W. (1974). Once Upon a Seesaw. *Harvard Business Review, 52*(2), 99–109.
17	2,3	1974	Hammond, J. S., III. (1974). Do's & Don'ts of Computer Models for Planning. *Harvard Business Review, 52*(2), 110–123.
16	1	1973	McFarlan, F. W. (1973). Management Audit of the EDP Department. *Harvard Business Review, 51*(3), 131–142.
15	5	1973	Davis, E. W., & White, L. (1973). How to Avoid Construction Headaches. *Harvard Business Review, 51*(2), 87–93.
14	1	1972	Vancil, F. R. (1972). Better Management of Corporate Development. *Harvard Business Review, 50*(5), 53–62.
13	6	1971	Jonason, P. (1971). Project Management Swedish Style. *Harvard Business Review, 49*(6), 104–109.
12	7	1971	Block, B. E. (1971). Accomplishment/Cost: Better Project Control. *Harvard Business Review, 49*(3), 110–124.
11	7	1969	Anderson, R. M. (1969). Handling Risk in Defense Contracting. *Harvard Business Review, 47*(4), 90–98.
10	1,7	1969	Saitow, A. R. (1969). CSPC: Reporting Project Success to the Top. *Harvard Business Review, 47*(1), 88–97.
9	4,7	1968	Howell, R. A. (1968). Multi-Project Control. *Harvard Business Review, 46*(2), 63–70.
8	6	1967	Morse, F. B. (1967). Private Responsibility for Public Management. *Harvard Business Review, 45*(2), 6–180.

(continued next page)

7	6	1967	Middleton, C. J. (1967). How to Set Up A Project Organization. *Harvard Business Review, 45*(2), 73–82.
6	4	1966	Cooper, A. C. (1966). Small Companies Can Pioneer New Products. *Harvard Business Review, 44*(5), 162–171.
5	1	1963	Levy, F. L., Thompson, G. L., Weist, J. D. (1963). *Harvard Business Review, 41*(5), 98–108.
4	7	1963	Dearden, J. (1963). Profit-Planning Accounting for Small Firms. *Harvard Business Review, 41*(2), 66–76.
3	1	1962	Miller, R. W. (1962). How to Plan and Control with PERT. *Harvard Business Review, 40*(2), 93–104.
2	2,6	1959	Gaddis, P.O. (1959). The Project Manager. *Harvard Business Review, 37*(3), 89–97.
1	1	1958	Roy, H.J. H. (1958). Operations Research in Action. *Harvard Business Review, 36*(5), 120–128.

California Management Review

Ref #	Class. Code	Year	Journal Articles
25	3,4,7	2007	Shi, Y. (2007). Today's Solution and Tomorrow's Problem: The Business Process Outsourcing Risk Management Puzzle. *California Management Review, 49*(3), 27–44.
24	2	2007	Skjølsvik, T., Løwendahl, B. R., Kvålshaugen, R., & Fosstenløkken, S. M. (2007). Choosing to Learn and Learning to Choose: Strategies for Client Co-Production And Knowledge Development. *California Management Review, 49*(3), 110–128.
23	1,2	2006	Cross, R., Laseter, T., Parker, A., Velasquez. G. (2006). Using Social Network Analysis to Improve Communities of Practice. *California Management Review, 49*(1), 32–60.
22	3,6	2004	Fichman, R. G., Keil, M., & Amrit Tiwana, A. (2007). Beyond Valuation: "Options Thinking" in IT Project Management. *California Management Review, 47*(2), 74–96.
21	2,3,7	2004	Iacovou, C. L., & Dexter, A. S. (2004). Turning Around Runaway Information Technology Projects. *California Management Review, 46*(4), 68–88.
20	2,3,7	2004	Kale, P., & Puranam, P. (2004). Choosing Equity Stakes in Technology-Sourcing Relationships: An Integrative Framework. *California Management Review, 46*, (3), 77–99.
19	2,7	2003	Hyer, N. L., & Brown, K. A. (2003). Work Cells with Staying Power: Lessons for Process-Complete Operations. *California Management Review, 46*, (1), 27–52.
18	3	2003	Day, G. S., Fein, A. J., & Ruppersberger, G. (2003). Shakeouts in Digital Markets: Lessons from B2B Exchanges. *California Management Review, 45*(2), 131–150.
17	3,7	2002	Soo, C., Devinney, T., Midgley, D., Deering, A. (2002). Knowledge Management: Philosophy, Processes, and Pitfalls. *California Management Review, 44*(4), 129–150.

(continued next page)

16	2,4	2002	Baron, J. N., & Hannan, M. T. (2002). Organizational Blueprints for Success in High-Tech Start-Ups: Lessons from the Stanford Project on Emerging Companies. *California Management Review, 44*(3), 8–36.
15	1,3	1999	Luftman, J., & Brier, T. (1999). Achieving and Sustaining Business-IT Alignment. *California Management Review, 42*(1), 109–112.
14	5	1999	Phelan, S. E., Lewin, P., Defillipi, R. J., Arthur, M. B., Hemphill, T. A. (1999). Letters to the Editor. *California Management Review, 42*(1), 180–194.
13	2,4	1998	Lynn, G. S. (1998). New Product Team Learning: Developing and Profiting from Your Knowledge Capital. *California Management Review, 40*(4), 4–93.
12	1,6	1998	Defillipi, R. J., & Arthur, M. B. (1998). Paradox in Project-Based Enterprise: The Case of Film Making. *California Management Review, 40*(2), 5–139.
11	4,8	1993	Price, M. J., & Chen, E. E. (1993). Total Quality Management in a Small, High-Technology Company. *California Management Review, 35*(3), 96.
10	1,4	1992	Rahrami, H., (1992). The Emerging Flexible Organization: Perspectives from Silicon Valley. California Management Review, *34*(4), 33.
9	6,7	1982	Drtina, R. E. (1982). Alternative Approaches to Complying with NEPA: A Cost Benefit Analysis. *California Management Review, 24*(4), 68.
8	4,6	1982	Schwartz, K. (1982). HP-Grenoble: Case Study in Technology Transfer. *California Management Review, 24*(3), 43.
7	2	1975	Harris, K. L. (1975). Organizing to Overhaul a Mess. California Management Review, *17*(3) 40–49.
6	1,3,6	1973	Powers, R. F., & Dickson, G. W. (1973). MisProject Management: Myths, Opinions, and Reality. *California Management Review, 15*(3), 147.
5	2	1970	Melcher, A. J., & Kayser, T. (1970). Leadership Without Formal Authority: The Project Group. California Management Review, 13(2), 57.
4	2,5	1969	Avots, I. (1969). Why Does Project Management Fail? *California Management Review, 12*(1), 66.
3	1,5	1964	Williams, L. K., & Williams, B. C. (1964). The Impact of Numerically Controlled Equipment on Factory Organization. California Management Review, 7(2), 25.
2	4,5	1960	Hertz, D. B. (1960). Is Technology Degrading Research? California Management Review, *3*(1), 18.
1	1,4,6	1960	Freeman, R. J. (1960). Quantitative Methods in R&D Management. California Management Review, 2(4), 36.

Sloan Management Review
(Please note that we were only able to search the database up to 1997 for SMR)

Ref #	Class. Code	Year	Journal Articles
13	2,6	1997	Cusumano, M. A. (1997). How Microsoft Makes Large Teams Work Like Small Teams. *Sloan Management Review, 39*(1), 9.
12	4,6	1997	Anil Khurana, A., & Rosenthal, S. R. (1997). Integrating the Fuzzy Front End of New Product Development. *Sloan Management Review, 38*(2), 103–120.
11	1,2	1995	Martinez, E. V. (1995). Successful Reengineering Demands IS/Business Partnerships. *Sloan Management Review, 36*(4), 51–60.
10	3	1990	Abdel-Hamid, T.-H., & Madnick, S. E. (1990). The Elusive Silver Lining: How We Fail to Learn from Software Development Failures. *Sloan Management Review, 32*(1), 39–48.
9	6,7	1990	Beidleman, C.R., Fletcher, D., & Veshosky, D. (1990). On Allocating Risk: The Essence of Project Finance. *Sloan Management Review, 31*(3), 47–55.
8	3,4,6	1988	Randolph. W. A., & Posner, B. Z. (1988). What Every Manager Needs to Know about Project Management. *Sloan Management Review, 29*(4), 65–73.
7	6	1988	Gamble., M. I., Ten Dyke, R. P., Biggadike, E. R., & Nolen, W. (1988). Letters. Sloan Management Review, *29*(2), 5–6.
6	1,2,6	1987	Slevin., D. P., & Pinto, J. K. (1987). Balancing Strategy and Tactics in Project Implementation. *Sloan Management Review, 29*(1), 33–41.
5	1,2,4	1981	Edward B. Roberts, E. B., & Fusfeld, A.R. (1981). Staffing the Innovative Technology-Based Organization. *Sloan Management Review, 22*(3), 19–34.
4	2,6	1977	Thamhain, H. J. & Wilemon, D. L. (1977). Leadership, Conflict, and Program Management Effectiveness. *Sloan Management Review, 19*(1), 69–89.
3	2,6	1975	Thamhain, H. J., & Wilemon, D.L. (1975). Conflict Management in Project Life Cycles. *Sloan Management Review, 16*(1), 31–50.
2	6	1971	Crowston, W. B. (1971). Models for Project Management. *Sloan Management Review, 12*(3), 25–42.
1	2,6	1970	Gemmil, G., & Wilemon, D. L. (1970). The Power Spectrum in Project Management. *Sloan Management Review, 12*(1), 15–25.

Ref #	Class. Code	Year	Journal Articles
56	2,6	2006	Whittington, R., Molloy, E., Mayer, M., & Smith, A. (2006). Practices of Strategising/Organising: Broadening Strategy Work and Skills. *Long Range Planning,* (*39*)6, 615–629.
55	4	2006	Söderquist, K. E. (2006).Organising Knowledge Management and Dissemination in New Product Development: Lessons from 12 Global Corporations. *Long Range Planning, 39*(5), 497–523.
54	2,6	2004	Papalexandris, A., Ioannou, G., Prastacos, G. P. (2004). Implementing the Balanced Scorecard in Greece: a Software Firm's Experience. *Long Range Planning, 37*(4), 351–366.
53	5	2003	Doh, J. P., & Ramamurti, R. (2003). Reassessing Risk in Developing Country Infrastructure. *Long Range Planning, 36*(4), 337–353.
52	7	2003	Lubatkin, M. H., Schulze, W. S., McNulty, J. J., & Yeh, T. D. (2003). But Will it Raise My Share Price? New Thoughts About an Old Question. *Long Range Planning, 36*(1), 81–91.
51	4,6	2002	Kodama, M. (2002). Transforming an Old Economy Company Through Strategic Communities. *Long Range Planning, 35*(4), 349–365.
50	4,6	2002	Keegan, A. & Turner, J. R. (2002). The Management of Innovation in Project-Based Firms. *Long Range Planning, 35*(4), 367–388.
49	6	2002	van Veen-Dirks, P., & Wijn, M. (2002).Strategic Control: Meshing Critical Success Factors with the Balanced Scorecard. *Long Range Planning, 35*(4), 407–427.
48	4	2002	Richard Hall, R., & Andriani, P. (2002). Managing Knowledge for Innovation. *Long Range Planning, 35*(1), 29–48.
47	6	2002	Armistead, C., & Meakins, M. (2002). A Framework for Practising Knowledge Management. *Long Range Planning, 35*(1), 49–71.
46	4,6	2001	Shenhar, A. J., Dvir, D., Levy, O., & Maltz, A. C. (2001). Project Success: A Multidimensional Strategic Concept. *Long Range Planning, 34*(6), 699–725.
45	4,6	1999	Gopinath, C. (1999). Investing in Newly Industrializing Economies: Managerial Lessons from the Enron Controversy. *Long Range Planning, 32*(3), 344–351.
44	7	1999	Cassells, E. (1999). Building a Learning Organization in the Offshore Oil Industry. *Long Range Planning, 32*(2), 245–252.
43	4	1996	Claxton, C. (1996). Creating a Global Newspaper. *Long Range Planning, 29*(5), 712–720.
42	4	1995	Töpfer, A. (1995). New Products—Cutting the Time to Market. *Long Range Planning, 28*(2), 61–78.
41	4,6	1994	Drew, S. (1994). BPR in Financial Services: Factors for Success. *Long Range Planning, 27*(5), 25–41.

(continued next page)

40	2,6	1994	Pellegrinelli, S., & Bowman, C. (1994). Implementing Strategy through Projects. *Long Range Planning, 27*(4), 125–132.
39	6	1994	Gadellaz, J. W. (1994). Avoiding Expensive Mistakes in Capital Investment. *Long Range Planning, 27*(2), 103–110.
38	6,7	1993	Grundy, T. (1993). Putting Value on a Strategy. *Long Range Planning, 26*(3), 87–94.
37	6,8	1993	Zairi, M. (1993). Competitive Manufacturing: Combining Total Quality with Advanced Technology. *Long Range Planning, 26*(3), 123–132.
36	5,6	1993	Lord, M. A. (1993). Implementing Strategy through Project Management. *Long Range Planning, 26*(1), 76–85.
35	1,6	1992	Roy, R., & Whelan, R. C. (1992). Successful Recycling through Value-Chain Collaboration. *Long Range Planning, 25*(4), 62–71.
34	4,6	1992	Siddall, P., Willey, K., & Tavares, J. (1992). Building a Transnational Organization for BP Oil. *Long Range Planning, 25*(1), 37–45.
33	4,6	1991	Mockler, R. J., & Dologite, D. G. (1991). Using Computer Software to Improve Group Decision-Making. *Long Range Planning, 24*(4), 44–57.
32	4	1991	Bates, D. L., & Dillard, J. E. (1991). Desired Future Position—A Practical Tool for Planning. *Long Range Planning, 24*(3), 90–99.
31	3,6	1990	Eden, C. (1990). Strategic Thinking with Computers. *Long Range Planning, 23*(6), 35–43.
30	6	1990	Calori, R., &. Atamer, T. (1990). How French Managers Deal with Radical Change. *Long Range Planning, 23*(6), 44–55.
29	5,6	1990	Stannard, C. J. (1990). Managing a Mega-Project—The Channel Tunnel. *Long Range Planning, 23*(5), 49–62.
28	3,6	1990	Yoo, S., & Choi, H. J. (1990). Managing on the Computer at a Korean Insurance Company. *Long Range Planning, 23*(2), 69–78.
27	3,6	1987	Babington, E. A. (1987). Installing a Computerized Planning System in Ghana. *Long Range Planning, 20*(4), 1987, 110–117.
26	1	1987	Joynt, P. (1987). Planning for the Older Manager—Collaborative Research in Norwegian Business. *Long Range Planning, 20*(3), 35–44.
25	3,6	1986	Tozer, E. E. (1986). Developing Strategies for Management Information Systems. *Long Range Planning, 19*(4), 31–40.
24	6	1986	Mason, J. (1986). Developing Strategic Thinking. *Long Range Planning, 19*(3), 72–80.
23	6	1986	Armenakis, A. A. , & Burdg, H. B. (1986). Planning for Growth. *Long Range Planning, 19*(3), 93–102.
22	1,6	1986	Pinnell, B. (1986). Keeping Corporate Planning Relevant—A Key Task for the Planning Department. *Long Range Planning, 19*(1), 45–51.

(continued next page)

21	6	1985	Chapman, A. (1985). From Organization Development to Corporate Development at Trebor. *Long Range Planning*, *18*(4), 50–54.
20	6	1984	TenDam, H., & Siffert, C. (1984). Strategic Management in a Firm of Consulting Engineers. *Long Range Planning*, *17*(4), 21–29.
19	1,6	1984	Kono, T. (1984). Long Range Planning of U.K. and Japanese Corporations—A Comparative Study. *Long Range Planning*, *17*(2), 58–76.
18	1,6	1983	Easterby-Smith, M., & Davies, J. (1983). Developing Strategic Thinking. *Long Range Planning*, *16*(4), 39–48.
17	6	1983	Lanford, H. W., & McCann, T. M. (1983). Effective Planning and Control of Large Projects—Using Work Breakdown Structure. *Long Range Planning*, *16*(2), 38–50.
16	6	1982	Jones, H. G. (1982). Tetra Pak—A Model for Successful Innovation. *Long Range Planning*, *15*(6), 31–37.
15	4,6	1982	Burrows, B. C. (1982). Venture Management—Success or Failure? *Long Range Planning*, *15*(6), 84–99.
14	1,6	1982	Green, G. J. L., & Jones, E. G. (1982). Strategic Management Step by Step. *Long Range Planning*, *15*(3), 61–70.
13	1,6	1981	Das, R. & Mohanty, B. (1981). Choosing a Diversification Project in a Regulated Economy. *Long Range Planning*, *14*(2), 78–86.
12	6	1980	Snowdon, M. (1980). Measuring Performance in Capital Project Management. *Long Range Planning*, *13*(4) 51C55.
11	1,6	1980	Piper, J. A. (1980). Classifying Capital Projects for Top Management Decision-Making. *Long Range Planning*, *13*(3), 45–56.
10	4,6	1977	Yavitz, B., & Schnee, J. E. (1977). Managing the Impacts of Large Public Programs. *Long Range Planning*, *10*(1), 65–72.
9	6	1976	Kono, T. 1976). Long Range Planning— Japan-USA— A Comparative Study. *Long Range Planning*, *9*(5), 61–71.
8	6	1975	Bonfitto, M. T., Hager, R. B., & Lapointe, F. A. (1975). Resource Management Schemes. *Long Range Planning*, *8*(3), 46–53.
7	4	1975	Martyn, A. S. (1975). Some Problems in Managing Complex Development Projects. *Long Range Planning*, *8*(2), 13–26.
6	6	1974	Gummesson, E. (1974). Organizing for Strategic Management—A Conceptual Model. *Long Range Planning*, *7*(2), 13–18.
5	6	1972	Smil, V. (1972). Energy and the Environment—A Delphi Forecast. *Long Range Planning*, *5*(4), 27–32.
4	6,7	1972	Palma, F. (1972). Computerized Analysis of Capital Projects by DCF Techniques. *Long Range Planning*, *5*(4), 53–60.
3	4,6	1972	Peretz, D. (1972). R & D and Corporate Planning in Government. *Long Range Planning*, *5*(4), 67–69.
2	4,6	1972	Desai, A. V. (1972). Technology Management in Indian Companies. *Long Range Planning*, *5*(4), 70–72.
1	2,6	1970	Knoepfel, R. W. (1970). Establishing Corporate Objectives at Solvay. *Long Range Planning*, *2*(4), 11–22.

IEEE Transactions on Engineering Management
(data available only from 1998 to 2007)

Ref #	Class. Code	Year	Journal Articles
96	3	2007	Patnayakuni, R., Rai, A., & Tiwana, A. (2007). Systems Development Process Improvement: A Knowledge Integration Perspective. *IEEE Transactions on Engineering Management, 54*(2), 286–300.
95	1,3,8	2006	Pollack-Johnson, B. & Liberatore, M. J. (2006). Incorporating Quality Considerations Into Project Time/Cost Tradeoff Analysis and Decision Making. *IEEE Transactions on Engineering Management, 53*(4) 534–542.
94	3,7	2006	Farris, J. A., Groesbeck, R. L., Van Aken, E. M., & Letens, G. (2006). Evaluating the Relative Performance of Engineering Design Projects: A Case Study Using Data Envelopment Analysis. *IEEE Transactions on Engineering Management, 53*(3), 471–482.
93	5,6,7	2006	Gil, N., Tommelein, I. D., & Schruben, L. W. (2006). External Change in Large Engineering Design Projects: The Role of the Client. *IEEE Transactions on Engineering Management, 53*(3), 426–439.
92	1,3,6	2006	Tiwana, A., & Keil, M. (2006). Functionality Risk in Information Systems Development: An Empirical Investigation. *IEEE Transactions on Engineering Management. 53*(3), 412–425.
91	1,6	2006	Meixell, M. J., Nunez, M., & Talalayevsky, A. (2006). Activity Structures in a Project-Based Environment: A Coordination Theory Perspective. *IEEE Transactions on Engineering Management, 53*(2), 285–296.
90	2,3	2006	Faraj, S., & Sambamurthy, V. (2006). Leadership of Information Systems Development Projects. *IEEE Transactions on Engineering Management, 53*(2), 238–249.
89	3	2006	Sarker, S., & Lee, A. S. (2006). Does the Use of Computer-Based BPC Tools Contribute to Redesign Effectiveness? Insights From a Hermeneutic Study. *IEEE Transactions on Engineering Management, 53*(1), 130–145.
88	2,3,4	2006	Akgun, A. E., Byrne, J. C., Keskin, H., Lynn, G. S. (2006). Transactive Memory System in New Product Development Teams. *IEEE Transactions on Engineering Management, 53*(1), 95–111.
87	1,2,4	2006	Holtta-Otto, K., & Magee, C. L. (2006). Estimating Factors Affecting Project Task Size in Product Development-An Empirical Study. *IEEE Transactions on Engineering Management, 53*(1), 86–94.
86	6	2006	Grant, K. P, & Pennypacker, J. S. (2006). Project Management Maturity: An Assessment of Project Management Capabilities Among and Between Selected Industries. *IEEE Transactions on Engineering Management, 53*(1), 59–68.

(continued next page)

85	1,3,4	2006	Abdelsalam, H. M. E., & Bao, H. P. (2006). A Simulation-Based Optimization Framework for Product Development Cycle Time Reduction. *IEEE Transactions on Engineering Management, 53*(1), 69–85.
84	3,4,6	2005	Oshri, I., & Newell, S. (2005). Component Sharing in Complex Products and Systems: Challenges, Solutions, and Practical Implications. *IEEE Transactions on Engineering Management, 52*(4), 509–521.
83	6	2005	Williams, T. (2005). Assessing and Moving on From the Dominant Project Management Discourse in the Light of Project Overruns. *IEEE Transactions on Engineering Management, 52*(4), 497–508.
82	3,4,6	2005	Serich, S. (2005). Prototype Stopping Rules in Software Development Projects. *IEEE Transactions on Engineering Management, 52*(4), 478–485.
81	1,3,4	2005	Bharadwaj, A., & Tiwana, A. (2005). Managerial Assessments of E-Business Investment Opportunities: A Field Study. *IEEE Transactions on Engineering Management, 52*(4), 449–460.
80	4,6	2005	Dillon, R. L, Pate-Cornell, M. E., & Guikema, S. D. (2005). Optimal Use of Budget Reserves to Minimize Technical and Management Failure Risks During Complex Project Development. *IEEE Transactions on Engineering Management, 52*(3), 382–395.
79	3	2005	Ng, K. Y. K, & Lam, M. N. (2005). Workflow Analysis of an Information Technology Organization: The Case of the Operational Mode During a Time of Crisis. *IEEE Transactions on Engineering Management, 52*(3), 396–403.
78	1,4,6	2005	Cho, S.-H., & Eppinger, S. D. (2005). A Simulation-Based Process Model for Managing Complex Design Projects. *IEEE Transactions on Engineering Management, 52*(3), 316–328.
77	6	2004	Cleland, D. I. (2004). The Evolution of Project Management. *IEEE Transactions on Engineering Management, 51*(4), 396–397.
76	1,4	2004	Swink, M. L., & Calantone, R. (2004). Design-Manufacturing Integration as a Mediator of Antecedents to New Product Design Quality. *IEEE Transactions on Engineering Management, 51*(4), 472–482.
75	4	2004	Sachon, M., & Pate-Cornell, M. E. (2004). Managing Technology Development for Safety-Critical Systems. *IEEE Transactions on Engineering Management, 51*(4), 451–461.
74	5	2004	Love, P. E. D., Irani, Z., & Edwards, D. J. (2004). A Rework Reduction Model for Construction Projects. *IEEE Transactions on Engineering Management, 51*(4), 426–440.
73	4	2004	Astebro, T. (2004). Key Success Factors for Technological Entrepreneurs R&D Projects. *IEEE Transactions on Engineering Management, 51*(3), 314–321.
72	2,6	2004	Ramabadran, R., Dean, J. W., Jr., Evans, J. R., & Ratur, A. S. (2004). Testing the Relationship Between Team and Partner Characteristics and Cooperative Benchmarking Outcomes. *IEEE Transactions on Engineering Management, 51*(2), 208–225.

(continued next page)

71	3,6	2004	Davis, F. D., & Venkatesh, V. (2004). Toward Pre-Prototype User Acceptance Testing of New Information Systems: Implications for Software Project Management. *IEEE Transactions on Engineering Management, 51*(1), 31–46.
70	3,4	2003	van den Ende, J., & Wijnberg, N. (2003). The Organization of Innovation and Market Dynamics: Managing Increasing Returns in Software Firms. *IEEE Transactions on Engineering Management, 50*(3), 374–382.
69	3,6	2003	Keil, M., Rai, A., Cheney Mann, J. E., & Zhang, G. P. (2003). Why Software Projects Escalate: The Importance of Project Management Constructs. *IEEE Transactions on Engineering Management, 50*(3), 251–261.
68	6	2003	Greiner, M. A., Fowler, J. W., Shunk, D. L., Carlyle, W. M., & McNutt, R. T. (2003). A Hybrid Approach Using the Analytic Hierarchy Process and Integer Programming to Screen Weapon Systems Projects. *IEEE Transactions on Engineering Management, 50*(2), 192–203.
67	4,6	2003	Stummer, C., & Heidenberger, K. (2003). Interactive R&D Portfolio Analysis with Project Interdependencies and Time Profiles of Multiple Objectives. *IEEE Transactions on Engineering Management, 50*(2), 175–183.
66	4,6	2003	Liberatore, M. J., & Pollack-Johnson, B. (2003). Factors Influencing the Usage and Selection of Project Management Software. *IEEE Transactions on Engineering Management, 50*(2), 164–174.
65	1,5	2003	Touran, A. (2003). Calculation of Contingency in Construction Projects. *IEEE Transactions on Engineering Management, 50*(2), 135–140.
64	2,3	2003	Tan, B. C. Y, Smith, H. J., Keil, M., & Montealegre, R. (2003). Reporting Bad News About Software Projects: Impact of Organizational Climate and Information Asymmetry in an Individualistic and a Collectivistic Culture. *IEEE Transactions on Engineering Management.*
63	3,7	2002	Snow, A. P., & Keil, M. (2002). The Challenge of Accurate Software Project Status Reporting: A Two-Stage Model Incorporating Status Errors and Reporting Bias. *IEEE Transactions on Engineering Management, 49*(4), 491–504.
62	4	2002	Rice, M. P., Leifer, R., O'Connor, G. C. (2002). Commercializing Discontinuous Innovations: Bridging the Gap from Discontinuous Innovation Project to Operations. *IEEE Transactions on Engineering Management, 49*(4), 330–340.
61	1,4	2002	Meade, L. M., & Presley, A. (2002). R&D Project Selection Using the Analytic Network Process. *IEEE Transactions on Engineering Management, 49*(1), 59–66.
60	4	2001	Nellore, R., & Balachandra, R. (2001). Factors Influencing Success in Integrated Product Development (IPD) Projects. *IEEE Transactions on Engineering Management, 48*(2), 164–174.

(continued next page)

59	2,8	2001	Laslo, Z., & Goldberg, A. I. (2001). Matrix Structures and Performance: The Search for Optimal Adjustment to Organizational Objectives. *IEEE Transactions on Engineering Management, 48*(2), 144–156.
58	1,4	2001	Loch, C. H., Pich, M. T., Terwiesch, C., & Urbschat, M. (2001). Selecting R&D Projects at BMW: A Case Study of Adopting Mathematical Programming Models. *IEEE Transactions on Engineering Management, 48*(1), 70–80.
57	3,6	2001	Jiang, J. J., Klein, G., & Discenza, R. (2001). Information System Success as Impacted by Risks and Development Strategies. *IEEE Transactions on Engineering Management, 48*(1), 46–55.
56	6,8	2001	Pate-Cornell, M. E., & Dillon, R. L. (2001). Success Factors and Future Challenges in the Management of Faster-Better-Cheaper Projects: Lessons Learned from NASA. *IEEE Transactions on Engineering Management, 48*(1), 25–35.
55	2,6	2001	Browning, T. R. (2001). Applying the Design Structure Matrix to System Decomposition and Integration Problems: A Review and New Directions. *IEEE Transactions on Engineering Management, 48*(3), 292–306.
54	4,6	2001	Dickinson, M. W., Thornton, A. C., & Graves, S. (2001). Technology Portfolio Management: Optimizing Interdependent Projects Over Multiple Time Periods. *IEEE Transactions on Engineering Management, 48*(4), 518–527.
53	2,4	2001	Shim, D. & Lee, M. (2001). Upward Influence Styles of R&D Project Leaders. *IEEE Transactions on Engineering Management, 48*(4), 394–413.
52	4	2000	Tatikonda, M. V., & Rosenthal, S. R. (2000). Technology Novelty, Project Complexity, and Product Development Project Execution Success: A Deeper Look at Task Uncertainty in Product Innovation. *IEEE Transactions on Engineering Management, 47*(1), 74–87.
51	2,4	2000	Kruglianskas, I., & Thamhain, H. J. (2000). Managing Technology-Based Projects in Multinational Environments. *IEEE Transactions on Engineering Management, 47*(1), 55–64.
50	1,6	2000	Machacha, L. L., & Bhattacharya, P. (2000). A Fuzzy-Logic-Based Approach to Project Selection. *IEEE Transactions on Engineering Management, 47*(1), 65–73.
49	6,8	2000	Paquin, J. P., Couillard, J., & Ferrand, D. J. (2000). Assessing and Controlling the Quality of a Project End Product: The Earned Quality Method. *IEEE Transactions on Engineering Management, 47*(1), 88–87.
48	1,4	2000	Ringuest, J. L., Graves, S. B., & Case, R. H. (2000). Conditional Stochastic Dominance in R&D Portfolio Selection. *IEEE Transactions on Engineering Management, 47*(4), 478–484.
47	1,2	2000	Heller, T. (2000). "If Only We'd Known Sooner" Developing Knowledge of Organizational Changes Earlier in the Product Development Process. *IEEE Transactions on Engineering Management, 47*(3), 335–344.

(continued next page)

46	2,4	2000	Lynn, G. S., Reilly, R. R., & Akgun, A. E. (2000). Knowledge Management in New Product Teams: Practices and Outcomes. *IEEE Transactions on Engineering Management, 47*(2), 221–231.
45	1,3,4	2000	Nambisan, S., & Wilemon, D. (2000). Software Development and New Product Development: Potentials for Cross-Domain Knowledge Sharing. *IEEE Transactions on Engineering Management, 47*(2), 211–220.
44	2	2000	Componation, P. J, & Byrd, J., Jr. (2000). Utilizing Cluster Analysis to Structure Concurrent Engineering Teams. *IEEE Transactions on Engineering Management, 47*(2), 269–280.
43	6	2000	Fricke, S. E., & Shenbar, A. J. (2000). Managing Multiple Engineering Projects in a Manufacturing Support Environment. *IEEE Transactions on Engineering Management, 47*(2), 258–268.
42	4	1999	Henriksen, A. D, & Traynor, A. J. (1999). A Practical R&D Project-Selection Scoring Tool. *IEEE Transactions on Engineering Management, 46*(2), 158–170.
41	2,3,6	1999	JJiang, J. J., & Klein, G. (1999). Information System Project-Selection Criteria Variations Within Strategic Classes. *IEEE Transactions on Engineering Management, 46*(2), 171–176.
40	6	1999	Grover, V. (1999). From Business Reengineering to Business Process Change Management: A Longitudinal Study of Trends and Practices. *IEEE Transactions on Engineering Management, 46*(1), 36–46.
39	1,4	1999	Rusinko, C. A. (1999). Exploring the Use of Design-Manufacturing Integration (DMI) to Facilitate Product Development: A Test of Some Practices. *IEEE Transactions on Engineering Management, 46*(1), 56–71.
38	4,6	1998	Bordley, R. F. (1998). R&D Project Selection Versus R&D Project Generation. *IEEE Transactions on Engineering Management, 45*(4) 407–413.
37	4	1998	Lieb, E. B. (1998). How Many R&D Projects to Develop? *IEEE Transactions on Engineering Management, 45*(1), 73 –77.
36	3,6	1998	Kumar, A., & Ganes, L. S. (1998). Use of Petri Nets for Resource Allocation in Projects. *IEEE Transactions on Engineering Management, 45*(1), 73–77.
35	1,6	1998	Shenhar, A. J. (1998). From Theory to Practice: Toward a Typology of Project-Management Styles. *IEEE Transactions on Engineering Management, 45*(1), 33–48.
34	1,7	1997	Chi, T., Liu, J., & Chen, H. (1997). Optimal Stopping Rule for a Project with Uncertain Completion Time and Partial Salvageability. *IEEE Transactions on Engineering Management, 44*(1), 54–66.
33	2	1997	Grant, K. P., Baumgardner, C. R., & Shane, G. S. (1997). The Perceived Importance of Technical Competence to Project Managers in the Defense Acquisition Community. *IEEE Transactions on Engineering Management, 44*(1), 12–19.

(continued next page)

32	4	1997	Balachandra, R., & Friar, J. H. (1997). Factors for Success in R&D Projects and New Product Innovation: A Contextual Framework. *IEEE Transactions on Engineering Management, 44*(3), 276–287.
31	5	1997	Larson, E. (1997). Partnering on Construction Projects: A Study of the Relationship between Partnering Activities and Project Success. *IEEE Transactions on Engineering Management, 44*(2), 188–195.
30	2,3,4	1997	Osterlund, J. (1997). Competence Management by Informatics in R&D: the Corporate Level. *IEEE Transactions on Engineering Management, 44*(2), 135–145.
29	1,4	1997	Kurokawa, S. (1997). Make-or-Buy decisions in R&D: Small Technology Based Firms in the United States and Japan. *IEEE Transactions on Engineering Management, 44*(2), 124–134.
28	2,4	1996	Brockhoff, K. K. L., & Schmaul, B. (1996). Organization, Autonomy, and Success of Internationally Dispersed R&D Facilities. *IEEE Transactions on Engineering Management, 43*(1), 33–40.
27	1,4	1996	Cabral-Cardoso, C., & Payne, R. L. (1996). Instrumental and Supportive Use of Formal Selection Methods in R&D Project Selection. *IEEE Transactions on Engineering Management, 43*(4), 402–410.
26	1,2,4	1996	Hauptman, O., & Hirji, K. K. (1996).The Influence of Process Concurrency on Project Outcomes in Product Development: An Empirical Study of Cross-Functional Teams. *IEEE Transactions on Engineering Management, 43*(2), 153–164.
25	4	1996	Balachandra, R. (1996). A Comparison of R&D Project Termination Factors in Four Industrial Nations. *IEEE Transactions on Engineering Management, 43*(1), 88–96.
24	1,6	1996	Pulat, P. S., & Horn, S. J. (1996). Time-Resource Tradeoff Problem [project scheduling]. *IEEE Transactions on Engineering Management, 43*(4), 411–417.
23	4,6	1995	Nobeoka, K., & Cusumano, M. A. (1995). Multi-Project Strategy, Design Transfer, and Project Performance: A Survey of Automobile Development Projects in the U.S. and Japan. *IEEE Transactions on Engineering Management, 42*(4), 397–409.
22	3,6	1995	Keil, M., Truex, D. P., III, & Mixon, R. (1995). The Effects of Sunk Cost and Project Completion on Information Technology Project escalation. *IEEE Transactions on Engineering Management, 42*(4), 372–381.
21	2,4	1995	Green, S. G. (1995). Top Management Support of R&D Projects: A Strategic Leadership Perspective. *IEEE Transactions on Engineering Management, 42*(3). 223–232.
20	1,2,4	1995	Morelli, M. D, Eppinger, S. D., & Gulati, R. K. (1995). Predicting Technical Communication in Product Development Organizations. *IEEE Transactions on Engineering Management, 42*(3), 215–222.

(continued next page)

19	4,6	1995	Green, S. G., Gavin, M. B., & Aiman-Smith, L. (1995). Assessing a multidimensional measure of radical technological innovation. *IEEE Transactions on Engineering Management, 42*(3), 203–214.
18	1	1995	Kamrad, B. (1995). A Lattice Claims Model for Capital Budgeting. *IEEE Transactions on Engineering Management, 42*(2), 140–149.
17	4	1994	Brockhoff, K. (1994). R&D Project Termination Decisions by Discriminant Analysis-An International Comparison. *IEEE Transactions on Engineering Management, 41*(3), 245–254.
16	2,6	1994	Abdel-Hamid, T. K., Sengupta, K., & Hardebeck, M. J. (1994). The Effect of Reward Structures on Allocating Shared Staff Resources Among Interdependent Software Projects: An Experimental Investigation. *IEEE Transactions on Engineering Management, 41*(2), 115–125.
15	1,3	1994	Zhu, Z., & Heady, R. B. (1994). A Simplified Method of Evaluating PERT/CPM Network Parameters. *IEEE Transactions on Engineering Management, 41*(4), 426–430.
14	4,6	1994	Chun, Y. H. (1994). Sequential Decisions Under Uncertainty in the R&D Project Selection Problem. *IEEE Transactions on Engineering Management, 41*(4), 404–413.
13	6	1994	Bailetti, A. J., Callahan, J. R., & DiPietro, P. (1994). A Coordination Structure Approach to the Management of Projects. *IEEE Transactions on Engineering Management, 41*(4), 394–403.
12	1,4	1993	Schmidt, R. L. (1993). A Model for R&D Project Selection with Combined Benefit, Outcome and Resource Interactions. *IEEE Transactions on Engineering Management, 40*(4), 403–410.
11	2,6	1993	Kalu, T. C. U. (1993). A Framework for the Management of Projects in Complex Organizations. *IEEE Transactions on Engineering Management, 40*, (2), 175–180.
10	1	1993	McCahon, C. S. (1993). Using PERT as an Approximation of Fuzzy Project-Network Analysis. *IEEE Transactions on Engineering Management, 40*(2), 146–153.
9	1,2,6	1992	Ford, R. C., & McLaughlin, F. S. (1992). Successful Project Teams: a Study of MIS Managers. *IEEE Transactions on Engineering Management, 39*(4), 312–317.
8	2,3,6	1992	Dean, B. V., Denzler, D. R., & Watkins, J. J. (1992). Multiproject Staff Scheduling with Variable Resource Constraints. *IEEE Transactions on Engineering Management, 39*(1), 59–72.
7	1,3,6	1991	Deutsch, M. S. (1991). An Exploratory Analysis Relating the Software Project Management Process to Project Success. *IEEE Transactions on Engineering Management, 38*(4), 365–375.
6	6	1990	Pinto, J. K., & Mantel, S. J., Jr. (1990). The Causes of Project Failure. *IEEE Transactions on Engineering Management, 37*(4), 269–276.

(continued next page)

5	1,6	1990	Kernaghan, J.A., & Cook, R. A. (1990). Teamwork in Planning Innovative Projects: Improving Group Performance by Rational and Interpersonal Interventions in Group Process. *IEEE Transactions on Engineering Management, 37*(2), 109–116.
4	3	1990	Rowen, R. B. (1990). Software Project Management under Incomplete and Ambiguous Specifications. *IEEE Transactions on Engineering Management, 37*(1), 10–21.
3	6	1989	Larson, E. W., & Gobeli, D. H. (1989). Significance of Project Management Structure on Development Success. *IEEE Transactions on Engineering Management, 36*(2), 119–125.
2	3,6	1988	Badiru, A. B. (1988). Successful Initiation of Expert Systems Projects. *IEEE Transactions on Engineering Management, 35*(3), 186–190.
1	6,7	1988	Lee-Kwang, H. & Farrel, J. (1988). The SSD Graph: A Tool for Project Scheduling and Visualization. *IEEE Transactions on Engineering Management, 35*(1), 25–30.

Journal of Operations Management

Ref #	Class. Code	Year	Journal Articles
33	6	2007	Zwikael, O., & Sadeh, A. (2007). Planning Effort as an Effective Risk Management Tool. *Journal of Operations Management, 25*(4), 755–767.
32	6	2007	Bendoly, E., & Swink, M. (2007). Moderating Effects of Information Access on Project Management Behavior, Performance and Perceptions. *Journal of Operations Management, 25*(3), 604–622.
31	1	2007	Småros, J. (2007). Forecasting Collaboration in the European Grocery Sector: Observations from a Case Study. *Journal of Operations Management, 25*(3), 702–716.
30	4,6	2007	Naveh, E. (2007). Formality and Discretion in Successful R&D Projects. *Journal of Operations Management, 25*(1), 110–125.
29	6	2006	Simpson, N. C. (2006). Modeling of Residential Structure Fire Response: Exploring the Hyper-Project. *Journal of Operations Management, 24*(5), 530–541.
28	4,7	2006	Swink, M., Talluri, S., & Pandejpong, T. (2006). Faster, Better, Cheaper: A Study of NPD Project Efficiency and Performance Tradeoffs. *Journal of Operations Management, 24*(5), 542–562.
27	2	2006	Dilts, D. M., & Pence, K. R. (2006). Impact of Role in the Decision to Fail: An Exploratory Study of Terminated Projects. *Journal of Operations Management, 24*(4), 378–396.

(continued next page)

26	8	2005	Rungtusanatham, M., Forza, C., Koka, B. R., Salvador, F., & Nie, W. (2005). TQM Across Multiple Countries: Convergence Hypothesis Versus National Specificity Arguments. *Journal of Operations Management, 23*(1), 43–63.
25	1,6	2004	Pagell, M., & Melnyk, S. A. (2004). Assessing the Impact of Alternative Manufacturing Layouts in a Service Setting. *Journal of Operations Management, 22*(4), 413–429.
24	1,7	2004	de Treville, S., Shapiro, R. D., & Hameri, A.-P. (2004). From Supply Chain to Demand Chain: The Role of Lead Time Reduction in Improving Demand Chain Performance. *Journal of Operations Management, 21*(6), 613–627.
23	1,6	2001	Herroelen, W., & Leus, R. (2001). On the Merits and Pitfalls of Critical Chain Scheduling. *Journal of Operations Management, 19*(5), 559–577.
22	4,6	2000	Stock, G. N., & Tatikonda, M. V. (2000). A Typology of Project-Level Technology Transfer Processes. *Journal of Operations Management, 18*(6), 719–737.
21	1,4	2000	Tatikonda, M. V., & Rosenthal, S. R. (2000). Successful Execution of Product Development Projects: Balancing Firmness and Flexibility in the Innovation Process. *Journal of Operations Management, 18*(4), 401–425.
20	1,4	1999	Song, X. M., & Parry, M. E. (1999). Challenges of Managing the Development of Breakthrough Products in Japan. *Journal of Operations Management, 17*(6), 665–688.
19	4,6	1999	Swink, M. (1999). Threats to New Product Manufacturability and the Effects of Development Team Integration Processes. *Journal of Operations Management, 17*(6), 691–709.
18	1	1999	Flynn, B. B., Schroeder, R. G., & James Flynn, E. J. (1999). World Class Manufacturing: An Investigation of Hayes and Wheelwright's Foundation. *Journal of Operations Management, 17*(3), 249–269.
17	1	1997	Small, M. H., & Yasin, M. M. (1997). Advanced Manufacturing Technology: Implementation Policy and Performance. *Journal of Operations Management, 15*(4), 349–370.
16	1,4	1997	Hartley, J. L., B. J. Zirger, B. J., & Kamath, R. R. (1997). Managing the Buyer-Supplier Interface for On-Time Performance in Product Development. *Journal of Operations Management, 15*(1), 57–70.
15	1,6	1996	Özdamar, L., & Ulusoy, G. (1996). An Iterative Local Constraints Based Analysis for Solving the Resource Constrained Project Scheduling Problem. *Journal of Operations Management, 14*(3), 193–208.
14	1,6	1996	Pinder, J. P., & and Marucheck, A. S. (1996). Using Discounted Cash Flow Heuristics to Improve Project Net Present Value. *Journal of Operations Management, 14*(3), 229–240.

(continued next page)

13	1	1996	Mehrotra, K., Chai, J., & Pillutla, S. (1996). A Study of Approximating the Moments of the Job Completion Time in PERT Networks. *Journal of Operations Management*, *14*(3), 277–289.
12	1,6	1995	Pollack-Johnson, B. (1995). Hybrid Structures and Improving Forecasting and Scheduling in Project Management. *Journal of Operations Management*, *12*(2), 101–117.
11	1,3	1993	Westbrook, R. (1993). Orderbook Models for Priority Management: A Taxonomy of Data Structures. *Journal of Operations Management*, *11*(2), 123–142.
10	1	1990	Meredith, J. R., & Amoako-Gyampah, K. (1990). The Genealogy of Operations Management. *Journal of Operations Management*, *9*(2), 146–167.
9	1	1990	Mosier, C. T., & and Janaro, R. E. (1990). Toward a Universal Classification and Coding System for Assemblies. *Journal of Operations Management*, *9*(1), 44–64.
8	6,7	1987	Smith-Daniels, D. E., & Smith-Daniels, V. L. (1987). Maximizing the Net Present Value of a Project Subject to Materials and Capital Constraints. *Journal of Operations Management*, *7*(1-2), 33–45.
7	1,7	1987	Flores, B. E., & and Whybark, D. C. (1987). Implementing Multiple Criteria ABC Analysis. *Journal of Operations Management*, *7*(1-2), 79–85.
6	3	1986	Mertens, P., & Kanet, J. J. (1986). Expert Systems in Production Management: An Assessment. *Journal of Operations Management,*, *6*(3-4), 393–404.
5	1,6,7	1986	Shtub, A. (1986). The Trade-Off between the Net Present Cost of a Project and the Probability to Complete It on Schedule. *Journal of Operations Management*, *6*(3-4), 461–470.
4	1	1984	LaForge, R. L, Wood, D. R., & Sleeth, R. G. (1984). An Application of the Survey-Feedback Method in a Service Operation. *Journal of Operations Management*, *5*(1) 103–118.
3	1	1984	Rosenthal, S. R. (1984). Progress Toward the "Factory of the Future." *Journal of Operations Management*, *4*(3), 203–229.
2	1	1980	Buffa, E. S. (1980). Research in Operations Management. *Journal of Operations Management*, *1*(1), 1–7.
1	1	1980	Powell, Gary N., & Johnson, G. A. (1980). An Expectancy-Equity Model of Productive System Performance. *Journal of Operations Management*, *1*(1), 47–56.

Ref #	Class. Code	Year	Journal Articles
20	3,4	2006	Mitchell, V. L. (2006). Knowledge Integration and Information Technology Project Performance. *MIS Quarterly, 30*(4), 919–939.
19	3	1999	Sambamurthy, V., & Zmud, R. W. (1999). Arrangements for Information Technology Governance: A Theory of Multiple Contingencies. *MIS Quarterly, 23*(2), 261–290.
18	2,3,6	1996	Newman, M., & Sabherwal, R. (1996). Determinants of Commitment to Information Systems Development: A Longitudinal Investigation. *MIS Quarterly, 20*(1), 23.
17	3	1995	Keil, M. (1995). Pulling the Plug: Software Project Management and the Problem of Project Escalation. *MIS Quarterly, (19)*4, 421.
16	3,6	1995	Tractinsky, N., &. Jarvenpaa, S. L. (1995). Information Systems Design Decisions in a Global Versus Domestic Context. *MIS Quarterly, 19*(4), 507.
15	2,3	1990	Emery, J. C. (1990). The Management Difference: A Tale of Two IS Projects. *MIS Quarterly, 14*(3), 1–1.
14	3,8	1988	Abdel-Hamid, T. K. (1988). The Economics of Software Quality Assurance: A Simulation-Based Case Study. *MIS Quarterly, 12*(3), 394.
13	3	1988	Kim, C., & Westin, S. (1988). Software Maintainability: Perceptions of EDP Professionals. *MIS Quarterly, 12*(2), 166.
12	1,3	1987	Mahmood, M. A. (1987). System Development Methods—A Comparative Investigation. *MIS Quarterly, 11*(3), 292.
11	1,3,6	1987	Klein, G., & Beck, P.O. (1987). A Decision Aid For Selecting Among Information System Alternatives. *MIS Quarterly, 11*(2), 176.
10	3,7	1987	Zahedi, F. (1987). Reliability of Information Systems Based on the Critical Success Factors—Formulation. *MIS Quarterly, 11*(2), 186.
9	2,6	1986	Brittain, K., & Leifer, R. (1986). Information Systems Development Success: Perspectives from Project Team Participants. *MIS Quarterly, 10*(3), 214.
8	2,3	1986	Franz, C. R., Robey, D., & Koeblitz, D. R. (1986). User Response to an Online Information System: A Field Experiment. *MIS Quarterly, 10*(1), 28.
7	3,6	1984	Felix, R. G., & Harrison, W. L. (1984). Project Management Considerations for Distributed Applications. *MIS Quarterly, 8*(3), 161–170.
6	3,6	1984	Ahituv, N., Hadass, M., & Neumann, S. (1984). A Flexible Approach to Information System Development. *MIS Quarterly, 8*(2), 69–78.
5	3,6	1984	Meador, C. L., Guyote, M.J., & Keen, P. G. W. (1984). Setting Priorities for DSS Development. *MIS Quarterly, 9*(8) 2, 117–129.

(continued next page)

4	2,3,6	1984	Daniel Robey, D., & Markus, M. L. (1984). Rituals In Information System Design. *MIS Quarterly*, *8*(1), 5.
3	3,6	1983	Shomenta, J., Kamp, G., Hanson, B., & Simpson, B. (1983). The Application Approach Worksheet: An Evaluative Tool For Matching New Development Methods with Appropriate Applications. *MIS Quarterly*, *7*(4), 1–10.
2	3,4,7	1980	Zmud, R. W. (1980). Management of Large Software Development Efforts. *MIS Quarterly*, *4*(2), 45.
1	3,8	1978	Halloran, D., Manchester, S., Moriarty, J., & Riley, R. James Rohrman. Thomas Skramstad. (1978). Systems Development Quality Control. *MIS Quarterly*, *2*(4), 1–13.

Strategic Management Journal

Ref #	Class. Code	Year	Journal Articles
9	6	2005	Haas, M. R., & Hansen, M.T. (2005). When Using Knowledge Can Hurt Performance: The Value of Organizational Capabilities in a Management Consulting Company. *Strategic Management Journal*, *26*(1) 1–24.
8	6	2005	Ethiraj, S. K., Kale, P. K., Krishnan, M. S., & Singh, J. V. (J2005). Where Do Capabilities Come From and How Do They Matter? A Study in the Software Services Industry. *Strategic Management Journal*, *26*(1), 25–45.
7	6,7	2004	Zollo, M., & Singh, H. (2004). Deliberate Learning in Corporate Acquisitions: Post-Acquisition Strategies and Integration Capability in U.S. Bank Mergers. *Strategic Management Journal*, *25*(13), 1233–1258.
6	6	2001	Takeishi, A. (2001). Bridging Inter- and Intra-Firm Boundaries: Management of Supplier Involvement in Automobile Product Development. *Strategic Management Journal*, *22*(5) 403.
5	4,6	1999	Hoopes, D. G., & Postrel, S (1999). Shared Knowledge, "Glitches," and "Product Development Performance. *Strategic Management Journal*, *20*(9) 837.
4	1,6	1993	Bryson, J. M., & Bromiley, P. (1993). Critical Factors Affecting the Planning and Implementation of Major Projects. *Strategic Management Journal*, *14*(5) 319–337.
3	3,6	1992	Holland, C., Lockett, G., & Blackman, I. (1992). Planning for Electronic Data Interchange. *Strategic Management Journal*, *13*(7), 539–551.
2	2,4	1992	Leonard-Barton, D. (1992). Core Capabilities and Core Rigidities: A Paradox in Managing New Product Development. *Strategic Management Journal*, *13*(Summer, Special Issue), 111–125.
1	6	1987	Prescott, J. E., & Smith, D. C. (1987). A Project-Based Approach to Competitive. *Strategic Management Journal*, *8*(5), 411–412.

Administrative Science Quarterly

Ref #	Class. Code	Year	Journal Articles
3	2,6	1989	Burns, L. R. (1989). Matrix Management in Hospitals: Testing Theories of Matrix Structure and Development. *Administrative Science Quarterly, 34*(3), 349.
2	1,2	1971	Carter, E. E. (1971). The Behavioral Theory of the Firm and Top-Level Corporate Decisions. *Administrative Science Quarterly, 16*(4), 413.
1	1,2	1967	Burack, E. H. (1967). Industrial Management in Advanced Production Systems: Some Theoretical Concepts and Preliminary Findings. *Administrative Science Quarterly, 12*(3), 479.

Journal of Small Business

Ref #	Class. Code	Year	Journal Articles
1	2,6	1991	Larson, E. W., & Gobeli, D. H. (1991). Application of Project Management by Small Businesses to Develop New Products and Services. *Journal of Small Business Management, 29*(2), 30–41.

APPENDIX B

Research Trends of Eight Allied Disciplines from Top Management Journals

Operations Research, Decision Sciences, Operation Management, and Supply Chain Management (OR/DS/OM/SCM)

No.	Journal Name	1950-59	1960-69	1970-79	1980-89	1990-99	2000-07	TOTAL	%
1	AOM Executive	0	0	0	0	0	0	0	0%
2	AOM Journal	0	3	3	1	3	4	14	6%
3	AOM Review	0	0	1	3	1	3	8	4%
4	California Management Review	0	2	1	3	3	1	10	4%
5	Harvard Business Review	0	4	2	3	3	2	14	6%
6	IEEE Transactions on Eng. Mgmt	0	0	0	0	14	13	27	12%
7	Information Systems Research	0	0	0	0	2	1	3	1%
8	Interfaces	0	0	6	9	3	7	25	11%
9	Journal of Operations Management	0	0	0	6	11	5	22	10%
10	Long Range Planning	0	0	0	7	1	0	8	4%
11	Management Science	2	7	17	11	10	14	61	27%
12	MIS Quarterly	0	0	0	2	0	0	2	1%
13	Operations Research	1	3	6	3	8	3	24	11%
14	Organization Science	0	0	0	0	1	1	2	1%
15	Sloan Management Review	0	0	0	1	2	0	3	1%
16	Strategic Management Journal	0	0	0	0	1	0	1	0%
17	Journal of Small Business	0	0	0	0	2	0	2	1%
18	Administrative Science Quarterly	0	1	1	0	0	0	2	1%
	TOTAL	3	20	37	49	65	54	228	100%
	PERECENTAGE	1%	9%	16%	21%	29%	24%	100%	

Organizational Behavior and Human Resources Management (OB/HRM)

No.	Journal Name	1950-59	1960-69	1970-79	1980-89	1990-99	2000-07	TOTAL	%
1	AOM Executive	0	0	0	0	8	7	15	12%
2	AOM Journal	0	1	4	2	5	3	15	12%
3	AOM Review	0	0	0	1	2	2	5	4%
4	California Management Review	0	1	2	0	1	6	10	8%
5	Harvard Business Review	1	0	3	3	2	3	12	9%
6	IEEE Transactions on Eng. Mgmt	0	0	0	0	10	12	22	17%
7	Information Systems Research	0	0	0	0	3	0	3	2%
8	Interfaces	0	0	1	3	1	0	5	4%
9	J. of Operations Management	0	0	0	0	0	1	1	1%
10	Long Range Planning	0	0	1	0	1	2	4	3%
11	Management Science	0	2	3	0	4	3	12	9%
12	MIS Quarterly	0	0	0	3	2	0	5	4%
13	Operations Research	0	0	0	0	0	0	0	0%
14	Organization Science	0	0	0	0	1	4	5	4%
15	Sloan Management Review	0	0	3	1	3	0	7	6%
16	Strategic Management Journal	0	0	0	0	1	0	1	1%
17	Journal of Small Business	0	0	0	0	2	0	2	2%
18	Administrative Science Quarterly	0	1	1	1	0	0	3	2%
	TOTAL	1	5	18	14	46	43	127	100%
	PERCENTAGE	1%	4%	14%	11%	36%	34%	100%	

Information Technology and Information Systems (IT/IS)

No.	Journal Name	1950-59	1960-69	1970-79	1980-89	1990-99	2000-07	TOTAL	%
1	AOM Executive	0	0	0	0	1	0	1	1%
2	AOM Journal	0	0	0	0	0	0	0	0%
3	AOM Review	0	0	0	0	0	0	0	0%
4	California Management Review	0	0	1	0	1	6	8	8%
5	Harvard Business Review	0	0	1	1	0	0	2	2%
6	IEEE Transactions on Eng. Mgmt	0	0	0	0	8	13	21	20%
7	Information Systems Research	0	0	0	0	6	9	15	14%
8	Interfaces	0	0	0	2	1	0	3	3%
9	Journal of Operations Management	0	0	0	1	1	0	2	2%
10	Long Range Planning	0	0	0	2	2	0	4	4%
11	Management Science	2	2	3	2	6	7	22	21%
12	MIS Quarterly	0	0	1	12	5	1	19	18%
13	Operations Research	0	0	1	2	0	1	4	4%
14	Organization Science	0	0	0	0	1	0	1	1%
15	Sloan Management Review	0	0	0	0	2	0	2	2%
16	Strategic Management Journal	0	0	0	0	1	0	1	1%
17	Journal of Small Business	0	0	0	0	0	0	0	0%
18	Administrative Science Quarterly	0	0	0	0	0	0	0	0%
	TOTAL	2	2	7	22	35	37	105	100%
	PERCENTAGE	2%	2%	7%	21%	33%	35%	100%	

Technology, Innovation, New Product Development, and Research and Development (TECH/INNOV/NPD/R&D)

No.	Journal Name	1950-59	1960-69	1970-79	1980-89	1990-99	2000-07	TOTAL	%
1	AOM Executive	0	0	0	0	0	0	0	0%
2	AOM Journal	0	0	1	1	2	3	7	6%
3	AOM Review	0	0	0	0	1	1	2	2%
4	California Management Review	0	0	2	1	3	2	8	7%
5	Harvard Business Review	0	0	2	0	0	0	2	2%
6	IEEE Transactions on Eng. Mgmt	0	0	0	0	16	18	34	31%
7	Information Systems Research	0	0	0	0	1	2	3	3%
8	Interfaces	0	0	1	1	2	0	4	4%
9	Journal of Operations Management	0	0	0	0	3	4	7	6%
10	Long Range Planning	0	0	4	1	7	5	17	15%
11	Management Science	0	1	2	6	1	7	17	15%
12	MIS Quarterly	0	0	0	1	0	1	2	2%
13	Operations Research	0	0	0	0	0	1	1	1%
14	Organization Science	0	0	0	0	0	2	2	2%
15	Sloan Management Review	0	0	0	2	1	0	3	3%
16	Strategic Management Journal	0	0	0	0	2	0	2	2%
17	Journal of Small Business	0	0	0	0	0	0	0	0%
18	Administrative Science Quarterly	0	0	0	0	0	0	0	0%
	TOTAL	0	1	12	13	39	46	111	100%
	PERCENTAGE	0%	1%	11%	12%	35%	41%	100%	

Engineering-Construction, Contracts, Legal Aspects, and Expert Witness (EC/CONTRACT/LEGAL)

No.	Journal Name	1950-59	1960-69	1970-79	1980-89	1990-99	2000-07	TOTAL	%
1	AOM Executive	0	0	0	0	0	0	0	0%
2	AOM Journal	0	0	0	0	0	0	0	0%
3	AOM Review	0	0	0	0	0	0	0	0%
4	California Management Review	0	3	0	0	1	0	4	14%
5	Harvard Business Review	0	0	0	2	1	0	3	11%
6	IEEE Transactions on Eng. Mgmt	0	0	0	0	1	2	3	11%
7	Information Systems Research	0	0	0	0	1	0	1	4%
8	Interfaces	0	0	0	0	0	0	0	0%
9	Journal of Operations Management	0	0	0	0	0	0	0	0%
10	Long Range Planning	0	0	0	0	2	1	3	11%
11	Management Science	0	0	1	1	2	3	7	25%
12	MIS Quarterly	0	0	0	0	0	0	0	0%
13	Operations Research	1	1	1	1	2	1	7	25%
14	Organization Science	0	0	0	0	0	0	0	0%
15	Sloan Management Review	0	0	0	0	0	0	0	0%
16	Strategic Management Journal	0	0	0	0	0	0	0	0%
17	Journal of Small Business	0	0	0	0	0	0	0	0%
18	Administrative Science Quarterly	0	0	0	0	0	0	0	0%
	TOTAL	1	4	2	4	10	7	28	100%
	PERCENTAGE	4%	14%	7%	14%	36%	25%	100%	

Strategy, Integration, Portfolio Management, Value of Project Management, and Marketing (STRATEGY/PPM)

No.	Journal Name	1950-59	1960-69	1970-79	1980-89	1990-99	2000-07	TOTAL	%
1	AOM Executive	0	0	0	0	0	3	3	1%
2	AOM Journal	0	3	7	1	1	1	13	4%
3	AOM Review	0	0	2	2	0	1	5	2%
4	California Management Review	0	1	1	2	1	1	6	2%
5	Harvard Business Review	1	2	1	6	4	5	19	6%
6	IEEE Transactions on Eng. Mgmt	0	0	0	3	18	23	44	15%
7	Information Systems Research	0	0	0	0	1	0	1	0%
8	Interfaces	0	0	4	9	5	6	24	8%
9	Journal of Operations Management	0	0	0	2	4	7	13	4%
10	Long Range Planning	0	0	9	16	14	7	46	16%
11	Management Science	1	2	17	18	12	21	71	24%
12	MIS Quarterly	0	0	0	7	2	0	9	3%
13	Operations Research	0	2	3	3	9	1	18	6%
14	Organization Science	0	0	0	0	0	3	3	1%
15	Sloan Management Review	0	0	4	3	3	0	10	3%
16	Strategic Management Journal	0	0	0	1	3	4	8	3%
17	Journal of Small Business	0	0	0	0	1	0	1	0%
18	Administrative Science Quarterly	0	0	0	1	0	0	1	0%
	TOTAL	2	10	48	74	78	83	295	100%
	PERCENTAGE	1%	3%	16%	25%	26%	28%	100%	

Performance Management, Earned Value Management, Project Finance, and Accounting (PERFORMANCE/EVM)

No.	Journal Name	1950-59	1960-69	1970-79	1980-89	1990-99	2000-07	TOTAL	%
1	AOM Executive	0	0	0	0	0	0	0	0%
2	AOM Journal	0	0	1	0	1	0	2	3%
3	AOM Review	0	0	0	1	0	2	3	4%
4	California Management Review	0	0	0	1	0	5	6	9%
5	Harvard Business Review	0	4	1	0	1	4	10	15%
6	IEEE Transactions on Eng. Mgmt	0	0	0	1	1	3	5	7%
7	Information Systems Research	0	0	0	0	2	3	5	7%
8	Interfaces	0	0	1	0	0	1	2	3%
9	Journal of Operations Management	0	0	0	3	0	2	5	7%
10	Long Range Planning	0	0	1	0	2	1	4	6%
11	Management Science	1	1	6	3	2	6	19	28%
12	MIS Quarterly	0	0	0	2	0	0	2	3%
13	Operations Research	0	1	0	0	2	0	3	4%
14	Organization Science	0	0	0	0	0	0	0	0%
15	Sloan Management Review	0	0	0	0	1	0	1	1%
16	Strategic Management Journal	0	0	0	0	0	1	1	1%
17	Journal of Small Business	0	0	0	0	0	0	0	0%
18	Administrative Science Quarterly	0	0	0	0	0	0	0	0%
	TOTAL	1	6	10	11	12	28	68	100%
	PERCENTAGE	1%	9%	15%	16%	18%	41%	100%	

Quality Management, Six Sigma, and Process Improvement (QM/6SIGMA/PI)

No.	Journal Name	1950-59	1960-69	1970-79	1980-89	1990-99	2000-07	TOTAL	%
1	AOM Executive	0	0	0	0	1	0	1	6%
2	AOM Journal	0	0	0	0	0	0	0	0%
3	AOM Review	0	0	0	0	0	0	0	0%
4	California Management Review	0	0	0	0	1	0	1	6%
5	Harvard Business Review	0	0	0	1	1	2	4	22%
6	IEEE Transactions on Eng. Mgmt	0	0	0	0	0	3	3	17%
7	Information Systems Research	0	0	0	0	1	0	1	6%
8	Interfaces	0	0	1	0	1	1	3	17%
9	Journal of Operations Management	0	0	0	0	0	1	1	6%
10	Long Range Planning	0	0	0	0	1	0	1	6%
11	Management Science	0	0	0	0	0	0	0	0%
12	MIS Quarterly	0	0	0	0	0	0	0	0%
13	Operations Research	0	1	1	0	1	0	3	17%
14	Organization Science	0	0	0	0	0	0	0	0%
15	Sloan Management Review	0	0	0	0	0	0	0	0%
16	Strategic Management Journal	0	0	0	0	0	0	0	0%
17	Journal of Small Business	0	0	0	0	0	0	0	0%
18	Administrative Science Quarterly	0	0	0	0	0	0	0	0%
	TOTAL	0	1	2	1	7	7	18	100%
	PERCENTAGE	0%	6%	11%	6%	39%	39%	100%	

Appendix C

Survey

Impact on Project Management of Allied Disciplines

The Project Management Research Team led by Dr. Young Hoon Kwak and Dr. Frank T. Anbari at The George Washington University in Washington, DC, is conducting a nationwide research to identify the "Impact on Project Management of Allied Disciplines" funded by the Project Management Institute.

As part of our research, we would like you to participate in this timely and important study to explore the impacts, trends, and challenges of the field of project management. The survey will take about 10 minutes of your time. Please follow the instructions very carefully and answer every question. All responses will remain anonymous and your identity will not be revealed. Your participation is crucial to the success of this research.

When you are finished entering your answers, click the "submit" button at the bottom of the survey. Once you have clicked the "submit" button, your survey is finished, and you cannot go back and change the answers. Also, please do not exit until you have received the message indicating that your survey has been successfully submitted.

If you have any questions or concerns, please contact Dr. Young Hoon Kwak (kwak@gwu.edu) or Dr. Frank T. Anbari (anbarif@gwu.edu). Thank you for participating in this research.

I. Operations Research/Decision Sciences/Operation Management/ Supply Chain Management (**DS/OM**) refers to the discipline associated with quantitative decision analysis and management principles including various optimization tools and techniques, network analysis, resource leveling, simulation, etc.

    1. The following scale represents the impact of **DS/OM** discipline on project management (PM):

	Low						High
	1	2	3	4	5	6	7

Up to 1969
Between 1970 and 1979
Between 1980 and 1989
Between 1990 and 1999
Between 2000 and 2007
In the future

    2. The following scale represents the availability of information/ knowledge/research on **DS/OM** related to project management:

	Low						High
	1	2	3	4	5	6	7

Up to 1969
Between 1970 and 1979
Between 1980 and 1989
Between 1990 and 1999
Between 2000 and 2007
In the future

II. Organizational Behavior/Human Resources Management (**OB/ HRM**) refers to the discipline associated with organizational structure, organizational dynamics, motivation, leadership, conflict management, etc.

    3. The following scale represents the impact of **OB/HRM** discipline on project management:

	Low						High
	1	2	3	4	5	6	7

Up to 1969
Between 1970 and 1979
Between 1980 and 1989
Between 1990 and 1999
Between 2000 and 2007
In the future

4. The following scale represents the availability of information/ knowledge/research on **OB/HRM** related to project management:

	Low						High
	1	2	3	4	5	6	7

Up to 1969
Between 1970 and 1979
Between 1980 and 1989
Between 1990 and 1999
Between 2000 and 2007
In the future

III. Information Technology/Information Systems (**IT/IS**) refers to the discipline associated with the use of computers and computer systems to process, transmit, store, and retrieve information for better management decisions.

5. The following scale represents the impact of **IT/IS** discipline on project management:

	Low						High
	1	2	3	4	5	6	7

Up to 1969
Between 1970 and 1979
Between 1980 and 1989
Between 1990 and 1999
Between 2000 and 2007
In the future

6. The following scale represents the availability of information/ knowledge/research on **IT/IS** related to project management:

	Low						High
	1	2	3	4	5	6	7

Up to 1969
Between 1970 and 1979
Between 1980 and 1989
Between 1990 and 1999
Between 2000 and 2007
In the future

IV. Technology/Innovation/Research and Development (**TECH/ R&D**) refers to the discipline associated with the concepts of making innovative and technological improvements and the research and development of entirely new products, services, and processes.

7. The following scale represents the impact of **TECH/R&D** discipline on project management:

	Low					High	
	1	2	3	4	5	6	7

Up to 1969
Between 1970 and 1979
Between 1980 and 1989
Between 1990 and 1999
Between 2000 and 2007
In the future

8. The following scale represents the availability of information/ knowledge/research on **TECH/R&D** related to project management:

	Low					High	
	1	2	3	4	5	6	7

Up to 1969
Between 1970 and 1979
Between 1980 and 1989
Between 1990 and 1999
Between 2000 and 2007
In the future

V. Engineering and Construction/Contracts/Legal Aspects/Expert Witness (**EC**) refers to the discipline associated with the use and application of a broad range of professional expertise to resolve issues related to engineering and construction, contracts, expert witness, and their legal implications.

9. The following scale represents the impact of **EC** discipline on project management:

	Low					High	
	1	2	3	4	5	6	7

Up to 1969
Between 1970 and 1979
Between 1980 and 1989
Between 1990 and 1999
Between 2000 and 2007
In the future

10. The following scale represents the availability of information/knowledge/research on **EC** related to project management:

	Low						High
	1	2	3	4	5	6	7
Up to 1969							
Between 1970 and 1979							
Between 1980 and 1989							
Between 1990 and 1999							
Between 2000 and 2007							
In the future							

VI. Portfolio Management/Program Management/Strategy/Business Process Outsourcing/ Integration (**PPM**) refers to the concepts of organizing and managing resources to maximize profit, minimize cost, and support the overall strategy of the organization.

11. The following scale represents the impact of **PPM** discipline on project management:

	Low						High
	1	2	3	4	5	6	7
Up to 1969							
Between 1970 and 1979							
Between 1980 and 1989							
Between 1990 and 1999							
Between 2000 and 2007							
In the future							

12. The following scale represents the availability of information/knowledge/research on **PPM** related to project management:

	Low						High
	1	2	3	4	5	6	7
Up to 1969							
Between 1970 and 1979							
Between 1980 and 1989							
Between 1990 and 1999							
Between 2000 and 2007							
In the future							

VII. Earned Value Management/Project Control/Performance Management (**EVM**) refers to the concepts and techniques that measure project progress objectively by combining measurements of technical performance, schedule performance, and cost performance.

13. The following scale represents the impact of **EVM** discipline on project management:

	Low						High
	1	2	3	4	5	6	7

Up to 1969
Between 1970 and 1979
Between 1980 and 1989
Between 1990 and 1999
Between 2000 and 2007
In the future

14. The following scale represents the availability of information/knowledge/research on **EVM** related to project management:

	Low						High
	1	2	3	4	5	6	7

Up to 1969
Between 1970 and 1979
Between 1980 and 1989
Between 1990 and 1999
Between 2000 and 2007
In the future

VIII. Six Sigma/Quality Management/Process Improvement (QM) refers to the concepts of improving processes, minimizing defects, and reducing costs by implementing continuous improvement principles and specific measures and metrics.

15. The following scale represents the impact of **QM** discipline on project management:

	Low						High
	1	2	3	4	5	6	7

Up to 1969
Between 1970 and 1979
Between 1980 and 1989
Between 1990 and 1999
Between 2000 and 2007
In the future

16. The following scale represents the information/knowledge/research of research on **QM** related to project management:

	Low						High
	1	2	3	4	5	6	7

Up to 1969
Between 1970 and 1979
Between 1980 and 1989
Between 1990 and 1999
Between 2000 and 2007
In the future

17. How do you see trends of allied disciplines (DS/OM, OB/HRM, IT/IS, TECH/R&D, EC, PPM, EVM, QM) and their potential impact on project management in the future?

18. In what way do you expect the trends of allied disciplines will change project management?

19. How will project management as a discipline look like in the future?

20. How should the project management community change their mindset in response to the trends of the allied disciplines that you answered from question 1 through 16?

21. How do you see the impact of project management on allied disciplines in the future?

IX. Demographics

22. Education:
   a. High school degree
   b. 2 year associate degree
   c. 4 year bachelor degree
   d. Master's degree
   e. Doctoral degree
   f. Other (please specify) _____

23. Years of work experience:
   a. Less than 2 years
   b. 2 to 5 years
   c. 6 to 10 years
   d. 11 to 15 years
   e. 16 to 20 years
   f. More than 20 years

24. Occupation:
    a. Academicians (professor or researcher)
    b. Students
    c. PM practitioner
    d. Consultant/Trainer
    e. Other (please specify) _____

25. If you want to participate in random drawings for amazon .com gift certificate, please provide your email.

If you have any other comments, feel free to contribute. Thanks.

Appendix D

Survey Analysis

1. The following scale represents the impact of (DS/OM) discipline on project management:								
	Low			Medium			High	Rating Average	Response Count
Up to 1969	41.5% (34)	23.2% (19)	12.2% (10)	9.8% (8)	2.4% (2)	8.5% (7)	2.4% (2)	2.44	82
1970–1979	15.9% (13)	26.8% (22)	22.0% (18)	15.9% (13)	11.0% (9)	4.9% (4)	3.7% (3)	3.09	82
1980–1989	8.5% (7)	11.0% (9)	23.2% (19)	23.2% (19)	23.2% (19)	7.3% (6)	3.7% (3)	3.78	82
1990–1999	0.0% (0)	1.2% (1)	12.2% (10)	31.7% (26)	28.0% (23)	22.0% (18)	4.9% (4)	4.72	82
2000–2007	0.0% (0)	2.4% (2)	3.7% (3)	14.6% (12)	23.2% (19)	39.0% (32)	17.1% (14)	5.44	82
Future	1.2% (1)	0.0% (0)	2.4% (2)	11.0% (9)	12.2% (10)	26.8% (22)	46.3% (38)	5.99	82
	answered question								82

2. The following scale represents the availability of information/knowledge/research on (DS/OM) related to project management:								
	Low			Medium			High	Rating Average	Response Count
Up to 1969	50.0% (41)	20.7% (17)	12.2% (10)	8.5% (7)	7.3% (6)	1.2% (1)	0.0% (0)	2.06	82
1970–1979	24.4% (20)	26.8% (22)	20.7% (17)	13.4% (11)	12.2% (10)	2.4% (2)	0.0% (0)	2.70	82
1980–1989	9.8% (8)	18.3% (15)	22.0% (18)	26.8% (22)	17.1% (14)	6.1% (5)	0.0% (0)	3.41	82
1990–1999	2.4% (2)	2.4% (2)	18.3% (15)	30.5% (25)	28.0% (23)	17.1% (14)	1.2% (1)	4.35	82
2000–2007	1.2% (1)	2.4% (2)	2.4% (2)	15.9% (13)	34.1% (28)	29.3% (24)	14.6% (12)	5.26	82
Future	1.2% (1)	2.4% (2)	2.4% (2)	6.1% (5)	12.2% (10)	31.7% (26)	43.9% (36)	5.96	82
	answered question								82

3. The following scale represents the impact of (OB/HRM) discipline on project management:								
	Low			Medium			High	Rating Average	Response Count
Up to 1969	39.0% (32)	20.7% (17)	18.3% (15)	14.6% (12)	4.9% (4)	2.4% (2)	0.0% (0)	2.33	82
1970–1979	22.0% (18)	23.2% (19)	17.1% (14)	25.6% (21)	9.8% (8)	2.4% (2)	0.0% (0)	2.85	82
1980–1989	9.8% (8)	14.6% (12)	24.4% (20)	28.0% (23)	17.1% (14)	6.1% (5)	0.0% (0)	3.46	82
1990–1999	2.4% (2)	3.7% (3)	19.5% (16)	30.5% (25)	19.5% (16)	22.0% (18)	2.4% (2)	4.37	82
2000–2007	0.0% (0)	1.2% (1)	7.3% (6)	13.4% (11)	36.6% (30)	29.3% (24)	12.2% (10)	5.22	82
Future	0.0% (0)	0.0% (0)	3.7% (3)	4.9% (4)	15.9% (13)	40.2% (33)	35.4% (29)	5.99	82
answered question									82

4. The following scale represents the availability of information/knowledge/ research on (OB/HRM) related to project management:								
	Low			Medium			High	Rating Average	Response Count
Up to 1969	39.0% (32)	22.0% (18)	20.7% (17)	14.6% (12)	2.4% (2)	1.2% (1)	0.0% (0)	2.23	82
1970–1979	19.5% (16)	23.2% (19)	26.8% (22)	24.4% (20)	4.9% (4)	1.2% (1)	0.0% (0)	2.76	82
1980–1989	12.2% (10)	14.6% (12)	22.0% (18)	30.5% (25)	14.6% (12)	6.1% (5)	0.0% (0)	3.39	82
1990–1999	2.4% (2)	7.3% (6)	15.9% (13)	29.3% (24)	25.6% (21)	14.6% (12)	4.9% (4)	4.32	82
2000–2007	1.2% (1)	2.4% (2)	3.7% (3)	23.2% (19)	30.5% (25)	26.8% (22)	12.2% (10)	5.09	82
Future	1.2% (1)	2.4% (2)	0.0% (0)	13.4% (11)	17.1% (14)	29.3% (24)	36.6% (30)	5.77	82
answered question									82

5. The following scale represents the impact of (IT/IS) discipline on project management:									
	Low			Medium			High	Rating Average	Response Count
Up to 1969	**58.5%** **(48)**	14.6% (12)	15.9% (13)	11.0% (9)	0.0% (0)	0.0% (0)	0.0% (0)	1.79	82
1970–1979	30.5% (25)	**31.7%** **(26)**	13.4% (11)	17.1% (14)	4.9% (4)	2.4% (2)	0.0% (0)	2.41	82
1980–1989	9.8% (8)	15.9% (13)	23.2% (19)	**25.6%** **(21)**	17.1% (14)	8.5% (7)	0.0% (0)	3.50	82
1990–1999	1.2% (1)	4.9% (4)	7.3% (6)	25.6% (21)	**26.8%** **(22)**	24.4% (20)	9.8% (8)	4.84	82
2000–2007	0.0% (0)	2.4% (2)	2.4% (2)	6.1% (5)	17.1% (14)	**45.1%** **(37)**	26.8% (22)	5.80	82
Future	0.0% (0)	1.2% (1)	1.2% (1)	4.9% (4)	6.1% (5)	22.0% (18)	**64.6%** **(53)**	6.40	82
	answered question								82

6. The following scale represents the availability of information/knowledge/ research on (IT/IS) related to project management:									
	Low			Medium			High	Rating Average	Response Count
Up to 1969	**53.7%** **(44)**	20.7% (17)	7.3% (6)	17.1% (14)	1.2% (1)	0.0% (0)	0.0% (0)	1.91	82
1970–1979	**34.1%** **(28)**	26.8% (22)	14.6% (12)	15.9% (13)	6.1% (5)	2.4% (2)	0.0% (0)	2.40	82
1980–1989	13.4% (11)	17.1% (14)	20.7% (17)	**26.8%** **(22)**	17.1% (14)	3.7% (3)	1.2% (1)	3.33	82
1990–1999	1.2% (1)	7.3% (6)	14.6% (12)	**29.3%** **(24)**	18.3% (15)	23.2% (19)	6.1% (5)	4.50	82
2000–2007	1.2% (1)	1.2% (1)	2.4% (2)	17.1% (14)	18.3% (15)	**40.2%** **(33)**	19.5% (16)	5.49	82
Future	1.2% (1)	1.2% (1)	2.4% (2)	7.3% (6)	9.8% (8)	22.0% (18)	**56.1%** **(46)**	6.13	82
	answered question								82

7. The following scale represents the impact of (TECH/R&D) discipline on project management:

	Low			Medium			High	Rating Average	Response Count
Up to 1969	31.7% (26)	28.0% (23)	18.3% (15)	15.9% (13)	2.4% (2)	1.2% (1)	2.4% (2)	2.43	82
1970–1979	19.5% (16)	24.4% (20)	28.0% (23)	14.6% (12)	9.8% (8)	2.4% (2)	1.2% (1)	2.83	82
1980–1989	7.3% (6)	12.2% (10)	29.3% (24)	25.6% (21)	15.9% (13)	7.3% (6)	2.4% (2)	3.62	82
1990–1999	0.0% (0)	3.7% (3)	19.5% (16)	28.0% (23)	24.4% (20)	18.3% (15)	6.1% (5)	4.52	82
2000–2007	0.0% (0)	2.4% (2)	7.3% (6)	19.5% (16)	22.0% (18)	26.8% (22)	22.0% (18)	5.29	82
Future	0.0% (0)	2.4% (2)	3.7% (3)	7.3% (6)	20.7% (17)	22.0% (18)	43.9% (36)	5.88	82
	answered question								82

8. The following scale represents the availability of information/knowledge/research on (TECH/R&D) related to project management:

	Low			Medium			High	Rating Average	Response Count
Up to 1969	35.4% (29)	35.4% (29)	9.8% (8)	14.6% (12)	3.7% (3)	1.2% (1)	0.0% (0)	2.20	82
1970–1979	18.3% (15)	37.8% (31)	20.7% (17)	12.2% (10)	9.8% (8)	1.2% (1)	0.0% (0)	2.61	82
1980–1989	7.3% (6)	18.3% (15)	31.7% (26)	25.6% (21)	11.0% (9)	4.9% (4)	1.2% (1)	3.34	82
1990–1999	1.2% (1)	2.4% (2)	20.7% (17)	36.6% (30)	17.1% (14)	17.1% (14)	4.9% (4)	4.37	82
2000–2007	1.2% (1)	0.0% (0)	4.9% (4)	23.2% (19)	24.4% (20)	30.5% (25)	15.9% (13)	5.24	82
Future	1.2% (1)	0.0% (0)	4.9% (4)	8.5% (7)	20.7% (17)	28.0% (23)	36.6% (30)	5.78	82
	answered question								82

9. The following scale represents the impact of (EC) discipline on project management:								
	Low			Medium			High	Rating Average	Response Count
Up to 1969	25.6% (21)	17.1% (14)	9.8% (8)	**26.8%** **(22)**	8.5% (7)	6.1% (5)	6.1% (5)	3.18	82
1970– 1979	11.0% (9)	22.0% (18)	9.8% (8)	**29.3%** **(24)**	13.4% (11)	9.8% (8)	4.9% (4)	3.61	82
1980– 1989	7.3% (6)	11.0% (9)	12.2% (10)	**28.0%** **(23)**	18.3% (15)	17.1% (14)	6.1% (5)	4.15	82
1990– 1999	1.2% (1)	3.7% (3)	8.5% (7)	**31.7%** **(26)**	23.2% (19)	22.0% (18)	9.8% (8)	4.77	82
2000– 2007	2.4% (2)	1.2% (1)	8.5% (7)	15.9% (13)	19.5% (16)	**31.7%** **(26)**	20.7% (17)	5.27	82
Future	2.4% (2)	1.2% (1)	7.3% (6)	11.0% (9)	14.6% (12)	23.2% (19)	**40.2%** **(33)**	5.65	82
answered question									82

10. The following scale represents the availability of information/knowledge/research on (EC) related to project management:								
	Low			Medium			High	Rating Average	Response Count
Up to 1969	24.4% (20)	17.1% (14)	17.1% (14)	**25.6%** **(21)**	11.0% (9)	2.4% (2)	2.4% (2)	2.99	82
1970– 1979	9.8% (8)	22.0% (18)	18.3% (15)	**25.6%** **(21)**	17.1% (14)	4.9% (4)	2.4% (2)	3.43	82
1980– 1989	7.3% (6)	7.3% (6)	14.6% (12)	**29.3%** **(24)**	20.7% (17)	18.3% (15)	2.4% (2)	4.13	82
1990– 1999	3.7% (3)	1.2% (1)	6.1% (5)	26.8% (22)	**30.5%** **(25)**	28.0% (23)	3.7% (3)	4.78	82
2000– 2007	2.4% (2)	1.2% (1)	3.7% (3)	12.2% (10)	20.7% (17)	**43.9%** **(36)**	15.9% (13)	5.43	82
Future	2.4% (2)	1.2% (1)	1.2% (1)	11.0% (9)	12.2% (10)	35.4% (29)	**36.6%** **(30)**	5.82	82
answered question									82

11. The following scale represents the impact of (PPM) discipline on project management:								
	Low			Medium			High	Rating Average	Response Count
Up to 1969	**43.9%** **(36)**	24.4% (20)	15.9% (13)	11.0% (9)	2.4% (2)	2.4% (2)	0.0% (0)	2.11	82
1970–1979	26.8% (22)	**29.3%** **(24)**	17.1% (14)	20.7% (17)	2.4% (2)	3.7% (3)	0.0% (0)	2.54	82
1980–1989	15.9% (13)	17.1% (14)	22.0% (18)	**23.2%** **(19)**	17.1% (14)	4.9% (4)	0.0% (0)	3.23	82
1990–1999	1.2% (1)	8.5% (7)	9.8% (8)	**32.9%** **(27)**	30.5% (25)	17.1% (14)	0.0% (0)	4.34	82
2000–2007	0.0% (0)	2.4% (2)	3.7% (3)	17.1% (14)	23.2% (19)	**35.4%** **(29)**	18.3% (15)	5.40	82
Future	0.0% (0)	0.0% (0)	2.4% (2)	4.9% (4)	12.2% (10)	31.7% (26)	**48.8%** **(40)**	6.20	82
answered question									82

12. The following scale represents the availability of information/knowledge/research on (PPM) related to project management:								
	Low			Medium			High	Rating Average	Response Count
Up to 1969	**53.7%** **(44)**	17.1% (14)	15.9% (13)	11.0% (9)	2.4% (2)	0.0% (0)	0.0% (0)	1.91	82
1970–1979	**37.8%** **(31)**	22.0% (18)	18.3% (15)	17.1% (14)	4.9% (4)	0.0% (0)	0.0% (0)	2.29	82
1980–1989	22.0% (18)	22.0% (18)	12.2% (10)	**26.8%** **(22)**	14.6% (12)	2.4% (2)	0.0% (0)	2.98	82
1990–1999	0.0% (0)	11.0% (9)	19.5% (16)	**26.8%** **(22)**	24.4% (20)	18.3% (15)	0.0% (0)	4.20	82
2000–2007	0.0% (0)	1.2% (1)	4.9% (4)	26.8% (22)	19.5% (16)	**34.1%** **(28)**	13.4% (11)	5.21	82
Future	0.0% (0)	0.0% (0)	3.7% (3)	6.1% (5)	14.6% (12)	25.6% (21)	**50.0%** **(41)**	6.12	82
answered question									82

13. The following scale represents the impact of (EVM) discipline on project management:

	Low			Medium			High	Rating Average	Response Count
Up to 1969	46.3% (38)	24.4% (20)	13.4% (11)	12.2% (10)	2.4% (2)	0.0% (0)	1.2% (1)	2.05	82
1970–1979	36.6% (30)	17.1% (14)	18.3% (15)	18.3% (15)	8.5% (7)	0.0% (0)	1.2% (1)	2.50	82
1980–1989	17.1% (14)	19.5% (16)	19.5% (16)	18.3% (15)	18.3% (15)	6.1% (5)	1.2% (1)	3.24	82
1990–1999	2.4% (2)	3.7% (3)	15.9% (13)	28.0% (23)	25.6% (21)	18.3% (15)	6.1% (5)	4.50	82
2000–2007	0.0% (0)	1.2% (1)	7.3% (6)	12.2% (10)	23.2% (19)	32.9% (27)	23.2% (19)	5.49	82
Future	1.2% (1)	1.2% (1)	1.2% (1)	7.3% (6)	12.2% (10)	25.6% (21)	51.2% (42)	6.10	82
				answered question					82

14. The following scale represents the availability of information/knowledge/ research on (EVM) related to project management:

	Low			Medium			High	Rating Average	Response Count
Up to 1969	51.2% (42)	24.4% (20)	11.0% (9)	11.0% (9)	1.2% (1)	0.0% (0)	1.2% (1)	1.91	82
1970–1979	39.0% (32)	19.5% (16)	17.1% (14)	14.6% (12)	8.5% (7)	0.0% (0)	1.2% (1)	2.39	82
1980–1989	23.2% (19)	15.9% (13)	17.1% (14)	22.0% (18)	17.1% (14)	3.7% (3)	1.2% (1)	3.10	82
1990–1999	1.2% (1)	9.8% (8)	17.1% (14)	23.2% (19)	23.2% (19)	22.0% (18)	3.7% (3)	4.38	82
2000–2007	0.0% (0)	1.2% (1)	6.1% (5)	14.6% (12)	28.0% (23)	24.4% (20)	25.6% (21)	5.45	82
Future	1.2% (1)	1.2% (1)	2.4% (2)	8.5% (7)	8.5% (7)	30.5% (25)	47.6% (39)	6.04	82
				answered question					82

15. The following scale represents the impact of (QM) discipline on project management:								
	Low			Medium			High	Rating Average	Response Count
Up to 1969	45.1% (37)	23.2% (19)	11.0% (9)	14.6% (12)	1.2% (1)	4.9% (4)	0.0% (0)	2.18	82
1970–1979	26.8% (22)	23.2% (19)	17.1% (14)	15.9% (13)	11.0% (9)	6.1% (5)	0.0% (0)	2.79	82
1980–1989	8.5% (7)	14.6% (12)	23.2% (19)	17.1% (14)	19.5% (16)	15.9% (13)	1.2% (1)	3.77	82
1990–1999	2.4% (2)	0.0% (0)	11.0% (9)	25.6% (21)	30.5% (25)	24.4% (20)	6.1% (5)	4.79	82
2000–2007	0.0% (0)	1.2% (1)	4.9% (4)	12.2% (10)	17.1% (14)	36.6% (30)	28.0% (23)	5.67	82
Future	0.0% (0)	1.2% (1)	1.2% (1)	9.8% (8)	12.2% (10)	23.2% (19)	52.4% (43)	6.12	82
	answered question								82

16. The following scale represents the information/knowledge/research of research on (QM) related to project management:								
	Low			Medium			High	Rating Average	Response Count
Up to 1969	50.0% (41)	19.5% (16)	11.0% (9)	15.9% (13)	1.2% (1)	2.4% (2)	0.0% (0)	2.06	82
1970–1979	29.3% (24)	28.0% (23)	14.6% (12)	15.9% (13)	9.8% (8)	2.4% (2)	0.0% (0)	2.56	82
1980–1989	9.8% (8)	14.6% (12)	20.7% (17)	22.0% (18)	18.3% (15)	14.6% (12)	0.0% (0)	3.68	82
1990–1999	1.2% (1)	2.4% (2)	11.0% (9)	30.5% (25)	24.4% (20)	26.8% (22)	3.7% (3)	4.70	82
2000–2007	0.0% (0)	2.4% (2)	3.7% (3)	12.2% (10)	22.0% (18)	34.1% (28)	25.6% (21)	5.59	82
Future	0.0% (0)	1.2% (1)	1.2% (1)	9.8% (8)	15.9% (13)	22.0% (18)	50.0% (41)	6.06	82
	answered question								82

Authors' Biography

Young Hoon Kwak, PhD is a project management faculty member at The George Washington University's School of Business (GWSB). He earned his MS and PhD in Engineering and Project Management from the University of California at Berkeley, was a visiting engineer at the Massachusetts Institute of Technology, and taught at the Florida International University in Miami before joining GWSB. Dr. Kwak is currently serving as a specialty editor (associate editor) for the *Journal of Construction Engineering and Management*, a member of the editorial review board for *Project Management Journal*, a member of the international editorial board for *International Journal of Project Management*, and an elected member of the Construction Research Council for American Society of Civil Engineers. He is a two-time recipient of the Project Management Institute's Research Grant and has more than 50 scholarly publications in journals, books, book chapters, and conference proceedings in the area of project management, risk management, technology management, and engineering and construction management. For more information, visit his website at http://home.gwu.edu/~kwak (kwak@gwu.edu).

Frank T. Anbari, PhD, MBA, MS Engineering, PMP, PE, and ASQ Certified Six Sigma Black Belt, is a faculty member and past Director of the Project Management Program at The George Washington University's School of Business (GWSB). Dr. Anbari taught in the graduate programs at Drexel University, Penn State University, and the University of Texas at Dallas. He serves as member of the editorial boards of *Project Management Journal* (2000–present), *International Journal of Project Management* (2007–present), and *International Journal of Managing Projects in Business* (2007–present). Dr. Anbari served as Vice President–Education and Certification, Project Management Institute-College of Performance Management (2005–

2007), Chair, Project Management Academic Committee at GWSB (2006), member of the Editorial Board of *Quality Management Journal* (1993–1998), and examiner (1993–1995) and alumni examiner (1999–2000) for the Malcolm Baldrige National Quality Award. He gained extensive industrial experience serving in leadership positions at the National Railroad Passenger Corporation (Amtrak), Day and Zimmermann, and American Water Works Service Company. He has developed and taught seminars on project management, quality management, and the Six Sigma method for private industry and public sector organizations throughout North America and Europe. He conducts rigorous research, presents widely, and publishes extensively on significant, timely topics in project management, technology management, and the Six Sigma method. For more information, visit his website at http://home.gwu.edu/~anbarif (anbarif@gwu.edu).